W9-ADE-618

Learned Friends

Learned Friends

A Tribute to Fifty Remarkable Ontario Advocates, 1950–2000

Jack Batten with The Advocates' Society

Published in 2005 by

Irwin Law

Suite 501, 347 Bay Street

Toronto, Ontario, Canada

M5H 2R7

ISBN: 1-55221-107-X

Editor: Rosemary Shipton

Design: Heather Raven

Photo research: Catherine Hatt

National Library of Canada Cataloguing in Publication Data

Batten, Jack, 1932–

Learned friends : a tribute to 50 remarkable advocates, 1950–2000 / Jack Batten.

Co-published by: Advocates' Society.

ISBN 1-55221-107-X

1. Lawyers—Canada—History. I. Advocates' Society. II. Title.

KE396.O6B38 2005   340'.092'2713   C2005-903245-6

KF345.Z9A1 B38 22005

The Publisher acknowledges the financial support of the Government of Canada through the Book Publishing Industry Development Program (BPIDP) for our publishing activities.

Printed and bound in Canada.

1 2 3 4 5   09 08 07 06 05

Table of Contents

vii   Foreword
        The Honourable R. Roy McMurtry, Chief Justice of Ontario

ix   A Message from the Presidents

x   A Message from the Editorial Board

xii   Sponsors

(Profiles are organized chronologically, according to the year in which each advocate was called to the bar.)

Part 1 **1921–1932**   2   Cyril Frederick Harshaw Carson

4   Isadore Levinter

6   William Belmont Common

8   Joseph Sedgwick

10   Vera Lillian Parsons

12   Margaret Paton Hyndman

14   Ernest Cecil Facer

16   Roydon Ambrose Hughes

18   Mayer Lerner

20   John Josiah Robinette

22   Francis Andrew Brewin

24   Edson Livingston Haines

26   Bernard Cohn

28   Brendan O'Brien

Part 2 **1933–1949**   32   John Douglas Arnup

34   Dalton Gilbert Dean

36   Gordon Fripp Henderson

38   Henry Herbert Bull

40   Goldwin Arthur Martin

42   John Thomas Weir

44   John Mirsky

46   John Malcolm Robb

48   Willard Zebedee Estey

50   McLeod Archibald Craig

52   Allan Goodman

54   Charles Leonard Dubin

56   Walter Bernard Williston

58   Arthur Edward Martin Maloney

60   Sydney Lewis Robins

62   David Gondran Humphrey

64   Bert James MacKinnon

66 Charles Terrence Murphy

68 John Patrick Nelligan

Part 3 **1950–1964** 72 Fernand Laurent Gratton

74 Bernard William Hurley

76 Julia Verlyn LaMarsh

78 Phillip Barry Chaytor Pepper

80 John Douglas Bowlby

82 John Francis Howard

84 Alfred Anthony Petrone

86 Donald Finlay Sim

88 Pierre Genest

90 Elmer Walter Sopha

92 Douglas Kerr Laidlaw

94 William Bruce Affleck

96 Louis Henry Tepper

98 Ronald Joseph Rolls

100 Ian Gilmour Scott

102 John Sopinka

104 Paul Stephen Andrew Lamek

106 Acknowledgments

107 Sources

Foreword

I would like to congratulate The Advocates' Society and Jack Batten for the publication of *Learned Friends: A Tribute to Fifty Remarkable Ontario Advocates, 1950–2000.*

My career in the legal profession has been long enough to allow me to know, or have known, every advocate honoured by inclusion in this book. These advocates are indeed a remarkable group of individuals who represent a very diverse range of styles of advocacy. However, their success as advocates, in my view, had certain important common characteristics – integrity, careful preparation, and, for the most part, civility to the court and to their opponents.

The art of advocacy today is undoubtedly more challenging than ever. Both civil and criminal trials continue to be increasingly complex. At the same time, I believe that the art of the successful advocate is as important outside the court-room as during the conduct of the trial or other hearing. At the outset of any litigation, good advocates must establish proper relationships of trust with their clients. The advocacy skills required will be crucial in shaping the litigation and in encouraging clients to accept reasonable settlements in civil cases or to enter pleas in criminal cases.

In my opinion, a successful advocate is also one who is prepared to engage in service to the legal profession and the broader community, including the political process. As society becomes more diverse and complex, there will never be any shortage of need for the good advocate. In fact, every day the art of advocacy is being employed across the public spectrum, in parliaments, in places of worship, and on a broad and diverse range of platforms – indeed, everywhere people meet to listen to someone expounding on some subject of public importance.

However, since I first entered law school, I have encountered widespread misunderstandings of the true function of the advocate. One of the most common is related to the ancient and familiar question: "How can you possibly defend a guilty man?" It is often stated that ordinary citizens espouse some particular cause because they believe in it, but that advocates espouse a cause because they are paid to do so. Advocates must be prepared to engage more in public legal education in order to remove the traditional mysteries that often envelop the administration of justice.

My father was a successful advocate until his career at the bar was cut short by a serious illness more than fifty years ago. I still have quotations kept by him from one Thomas Fuller, an English scholar who, in 1630, wrote about the attributes of "The Good Advocate." The following are a few of his comments, which I believe are equally relevant today.

> "Surely the lawyer that fills himself with instructions will travel longest in the cause without tiring. Others that are so quick in searching seldom search to the quick."

> "He makes not a Trojan-siege of a suit but seeks to bring it to a set battle in a speedy trial."

> "Be not like Anaximenes, of whom it was said 'that he had a flood of words and a drop of reason.'"

"He joys not to be retained in such a cause where all the right in question is but a drop blown up with malice to be a bubble."

"He is more careful to deserve than greedy to take fees. He accounts the very pleading of a poor widow's honest cause sufficient fees."

The role of the advocate is the most public face of the legal profession. The reputation of the bar, generally, will continue to be related to the quality of our administration of justice, which in turn is directly related to the quality of advocacy before our courts and tribunals. I expect that celebration of the careers of "remarkable advocates" will help to maintain the finest traditions of our profession.

The Honourable R. Roy McMurtry
Chief Justice of Ontario
May 2005

A Message from the Presidents

Ontario has a long history of excellence in advocacy. The strength and the vibrancy of our justice system have in large part been due to the quality of advocacy in our courtrooms.

Much of our knowledge of great advocates of the past has, until now, depended on an oral tradition. Those who were fortunate enough to work with, observe, or litigate against those advocates have spoken of their successes, failures, habits, and idiosyncrasies to younger colleagues, who in turn have passed the stories on. As time has elapsed, however, the need for a permanent record has become apparent.

As part of its Fortieth Anniversary celebrations, The Advocates' Society determined to create a permanent tribute to talented advocates who are no longer actively litigating, as a way of acknowledging the significant contributions of remarkable men and women who, in pleading cases in courtrooms across our province, set the standards of excellence to which the current generation of advocates aspires.

The selection of advocates featured in this book was made by an Editorial Board comprised of leading advocates and jurists: Kevin R. Aalto, Sheila R. Block, J. Bruce Carr-Harris, The Honourable Justice Stephen T. Goudge, Brian H. Greenspan, Marie T. Henein, George B. Kilpatrick, The Honourable Justice Jean-Marc Labrosse, Paul F. Monahan, Chris G. Paliare, LSM, C. Scott Ritchie, QC, Charles F. Scott, James C. Simmons, QC, and Harvey T. Strosberg, QC, who were joined by the two of us. We are grateful to the board for its work. It had the daunting task of selecting fifty remarkable advocates, made ever so slightly easier by a decision that we would not include anyone currently practising actively before courts or tribunals or sitting as judges. Many outstanding advocates were considered, and final decisions were difficult. Some may argue that others could have been included. But there can be no contesting the fact that the fifty men and women featured in this book are among the most distinguished ever to have practised in Ontario. We are proud to present the stories of their remarkable careers.

The Advocates' Society is grateful to the Law Foundation of Ontario for its significant support of this project, and to the staff at Irwin Law for their enthusiastic participation. We also are grateful to the many lawyers and law firms who generously donated funds necessary to bring this project to fruition.

We hope this book will help to ensure that the best of our traditions are remembered. Every member of The Advocates' Society will receive a copy, and the book will have a wide distribution across the province so that members of the community have the opportunity to understand the contribution that these outstanding advocates – our Learned Friends – have made to our justice system.

Jeffrey S. Leon
Immediate Past President
The Advocates' Society
May 2005

Benjamin Zarnett
President
The Advocates' Society
May 2005

A Message from the Editorial Board

People love lists. In creating a list of fifty remarkable advocates who practised in Ontario between 1950 and 2000, the members of the Editorial Board engaged in considerable debate and discussion about the wide array of candidates who were recommended.

While the final list may not be one with which everyone will agree completely, we believe it represents a fascinating cross-section of advocates from all areas of Ontario who made their mark in the courts during the last half century.

At the inception of this project, we used *The Book of Great Advocates* as the working title. The word "great," however, caused endless discussion among the board's judges and lawyers, many of whom had divergent views of what constituted "great." After struggling with the definition, we concluded, at Sheila Block's suggestion, that "remarkable" was a better adjective with which to describe the candidates. The *Shorter Oxford English Dictionary* defines this term as "worthy of remark, notice or observation; hence, extraordinary, unusual, singular." While this word proved to be more flexible, the debate over the choice of the final fifty advocates was no less animated.

The Editorial Board considered three other criteria in selecting the candidates. First, they could not currently be active before the courts or administrative tribunals of Ontario. Second, they should have been in active practice before the courts at some time between 1950 and 2000. Third, they should have been recognized leaders of the bar in the community in which they practised. The board also strove to identify candidates in all areas of the province. At the end of the process, we determined that the final list was indeed a list of advocates who, in their own way, were remarkable and of whom we, as a profession, should be proud.

The board is very grateful to the people who assisted in this project with their insights and contributions. Among them are publisher Jeffrey Miller of Irwin Law, who enthusiastically partnered with us to produce this book; noted author and former lawyer Jack Batten, who heard about the project and decided immediately that he wanted to research and write the profiles, and noted author Christopher Moore, for his input during the early planning stage and particularly for his suggestions regarding the title of the book. The Editorial Board also had the unending support and assistance of the staff of The Advocates' Society. In particular, we wish to thank Sonia Holiad, who diligently and persistently organized meetings of the Editorial Board and arranged all of the other elements and endless details that brought this very worthwhile project to fruition.

We hope you enjoy reading about these remarkable advocates who have contributed much to the rich legal history of our province.

The Editorial Board

Sponsors

The Advocates' Society is grateful for the support of The Law Foundation of Ontario

PATRONS ($10,000 +)

Borden Ladner Gervais LLP
Fasken Martineau DuMoulin LLP
Gowling Lafleur Henderson LLP
Stikeman Elliott LLP
Torys LLP
WeirFoulds LLP

BENEFACTORS ($5,000 - $9,999)

Goodmans LLP
Heenan Blaikie LLP
Lax O'Sullivan Scott LLP
Lenczner Slaght Royce Smith Griffin LLP
McCarthy Tétrault LLP
Sim Hughes Ashton & McKay LLP / Sim & McBurney

SUPPORTERS ($2,500 - $4,999)

Blake, Cassels & Graydon LLP
Bogoroch & Associates
Dimock Stratton LLP
Greenspan Humphrey Lavine
Mark D. Lerner
Lerners LLP
Nelligan O'Brien Payne LLP
Paliare Roland Rosenberg Rothstein LLP
Rogers, Moore
Sutts, Strosberg LLP

FRIENDS ($1,000 - $2,499)

Affleck Greene Orr LLP
Daniel & Partners LLP
Flaherty Dow Elliott & McCarthy
Forbes Chochla LLP
Fraser Milner Casgrain LLP

Genest Murray
Greenspan, White
Levinter & Levinter
McLeish Orlando LLP
Oatley, Vigmond LLP
Williams, McEnery

CONTRIBUTORS ($500 - $999)

Sheila R. Block
Filion Wakely Thorup Angeletti LLP
Hobson, Taylor, Oldfield, Greaves & D'Agostino
McCague, Peacock, Borlack, McInnis & Lloyd LLP
Sullivan, Pavoni, Patton, DiVincenzo
John C. Walker, QC

DONORS (UNDER $500)

Anthony J. Bedard
Birnie Associates
Ian T. Dantzer
Peter N. Downs
Murray N. Ellies, QC
Nigel G. Gilby
John W. Judson
Peter W. Kryworuk
Lucenti, Orlando & Ellies LLP
Joseph J. Masterson
Kimberley K. Munro
Kevin L. Ross
Stephen R. Schenke
Weaver, Simmons LLP

Part One

1921-1932

Cyril Frederick Harshaw Carson (1900–1980)

William N. Tilley spotted something bright and promising in the adolescent boy who showed up in his Toronto office one day in November 1916.

Tilley was arguably the leading civil litigator in Canada during the first half of the twentieth century. The lad he accepted as a student-at-law that day was sixteen-year-old Cyril Carson. A matriculant, Carson went to Tilley straight from high school and divided his learning time between office duties and Osgoode Hall lectures. This seemingly humble background didn't stop Carson from winning the gold medal in 1921, the year of his call to the bar.

On graduation, Carson joined the Tilley firm, where he worked for years as the great man's junior and slowly built his own career in the courts. There, he eventually rivalled Tilley himself. Carson's approach to litigation was built on doggedness and painstaking preparation. When he appeared in court, both at trial and on appeal, he wrote out his argument in full and read it to the court without deviation. If a judge interrupted to ask a question, Carson patiently answered, then picked up his reading at the very word where he had left off. It was a trick he managed without ever losing the court's attention, as he went about the blunt business of building his case brick by brick. This approach was rooted in Carson's enormous sense of self-sufficiency: he took it for granted that he was the only person in any courtroom, judges included, who really understood the law in each case he argued.

Carson may also have been the first counsel who worked with an entourage. On his major trials and appeals, he organized juniors and students into a team that researched the law from every conceivable angle. Each person contributed

analysis and ideas. But there was no mistaking that Carson was the man in charge, the counsel who went into court and persuaded judges and juries of the worthiness of his cause.

One of Carson's frequent courtroom opponents in later years, Barry Pepper, compared the Carson team method to a military operation. "Cyril always reminded me of the Battle of Crécy," Pepper said, as much in admiration as in fun. "At Crécy, a general would gather a couple of hundred troops and say, 'Now, you lot stand in this square here. All of you point your bows and arrows over there, and when I take off my hat, fire!' That was how Cyril functioned."

With such tactics, Carson attracted a range of blue-chip clients. His firm tended to the legal issues of the CPR, the Bank of Nova Scotia, Falconbridge Nickel Mines, the Canada Permanent Trust Company, and Hiram Walker–Gooderham and Worts. Carson was the counsel who got first call from both the Ontario and the federal governments, no matter which party held power in Toronto or in Ottawa. He was especially effective in tax and constitutional cases, and he set the record among Canadian counsel for appearances before the Privy Council.

Always a leader in his profession, Carson was elected treasurer of the Law Society of Upper Canada in 1950 and held the position for a remarkable eight years. It was a tempestuous period at the Society, a time when the province's legal education was undergoing revolutionary reconfiguration. Carson favoured retention of the traditional system, but when the forces for change prevailed, he immediately switched sides. He went on to play a key role in the Osgoode Hall addition, which housed the freshly created Bar Admission course. Not for the first time in his career, Cyril Carson proved that, in matters of the law, he was an old dog who could learn new tricks.

Isadore Levinter (1898–1990)

It was a toss-up for Isadore Levinter whether he would go into medicine or law. So he studied both at the same time. He was still a teenager, the son of an Austrian immigrant who owned a furniture store at Spadina and Queen.

For a year, 1917–18, young Isadore took classes in both disciplines, a feat that was possible in those days. But the dual studies came to an end in second-year meds, when Levinter faced his first cadaver. He almost fainted at the gruesome sight. From then on, he stuck exclusively to law. He received his call to the bar in 1921 and embarked on a long and fruitful career as the great strategist among civil litigators.

It was Levinter who conceived what he called "the hopscotch method" of examining witnesses at discovery. He focused his questions on one area, then hopped to a second area, a third, and then reversed himself back to the first. The aim was never to let the witness get comfortable with a set story. In cross-examination, another piece of Levinter strategy was to hold back on the final question in a sequence. The premise for this rule was based on the counsel's uncertainty about what a witness might unexpectedly blurt out. "Always quit before you hammer in the last nail," Levinter warned, "because the last nail may blow you apart."

Levinter's manner in court was disarming. A dapper dresser – out of court he wore a three-piece suit, wing collar, a gold tie, and a fresh rose in his buttonhole – he impressed jurors and witnesses with his elegant gown, looking as though he had just bought it, his tabs and collar gleaming white. He was polite and gentlemanly, a man whom witnesses under cross-examination were inclined to trust implicitly – until Levinter surprised them when he moved for the jugular.

For the first decades of his practice, he concentrated on plaintiffs' work in personal injury cases. He was so successful, the bane of insurance companies and the Toronto Transit Commission, that insurers finally decided to get Levinter on their side. Thereafter, his firm had the unusual distinction of carrying on a mixed practice of both plaintiffs' and defendants' work. Levinter could switch gears with the best of counsel, and, in one remarkable instance, he even took on a high-profile criminal trial. His client was a man named Alex MacDonald, the less-well-known brother of the notorious criminal of the 1930s, Mickey MacDonald. Alex faced a charge of murder and, at his trial, the versatile Levinter won a verdict of not guilty. He was delighted at his success, but decided not to pursue more business in the criminal courts.

Levinter distinguished himself equally in his activities beyond the courtroom. He chaired the civil liberties committee of the Canadian Bar Association, and he served as president of Beth Tzedec Congregation. When he was elected a bencher in 1956, he became the first Jewish lawyer to hold the position, winning re-election until he became a life bencher.

For a boy who grew up as a city slicker, Levinter had a great fondness for nature and the outdoors. He was a dedicated fisherman, and he rode his horse every Sunday morning. But his most astonishing embrace of rural life came in 1941, when he bought a 100-acre working farm just outside Toronto's city limits. The farm included thirty head of milking cows, hogs, sheep, chickens, and a vegetable garden. Since Levinter knew nothing about milking cows or shearing sheep, he sent his son Benjamin to the Ontario Agricultural College. With his college-taught expertise, Benjamin tended to the farm problems – even as he later pursued his own outstanding career in the law. But the question remained: Why did Isadore Levinter buy the farm in the first place? The reason, he explained more than once, was that he wanted to have something to fall back on in case he couldn't make a living as a lawyer. On top of all his other fine qualities, Levinter was a man of such modesty that his own great success in the law amazed him.

William Belmont Common (1899–1984)

In 1964, at the end of Bill Common's long career in the Crown's office, he estimated that he had taken 10,000 cases to court. That number was no idle boast, but close to the actual count.

In his time, Common served as the Crown counsel at the assizes all over Ontario, and he took three hundred Court of Appeal cases each year. "I practically lived at Osgoode Hall," he said. And as counsel to the Liquor Control Board of Ontario for almost a decade, he turned up in court whenever the board was a party to the proceedings. Somewhere in this hectic schedule, he managed to squeeze in nine years as a member of the Parole Board.

Born in London, England, Common came to Canada at age six, and, before he was out of his teens, he was back in Europe fighting in the First World War. He flew in the Royal Air Corps and won decorations from both France and Great Britain for blowing up a heavily fortified dam in occupied territory. He entered Osgoode Hall Law School after the war, winning the bronze medal in the year of his call to the bar, 1923. He spent three years in private practice before joining the Attorney General's Office and launching himself on his crowded life of work.

Common said that he found a comfort level in the courtroom from the beginning. He had a strong sense of his own intellectual equilibrium, and almost nothing in the courts knocked

"My duty," Common said, "was not to seek a conviction, but to purely lay before the judge and jury the evidence in the Crown's possession leading to the violation of the *Criminal Code* on which the indictment was based."

him off balance. He took his job with great seriousness but liked to joke about himself. When he was asked to assume the prosecution of offences for the Liquor Control Board, he said, shrugging, "As far as liquor goes, I know nothing about it except by consumption."

He earned a reputation as the most just of Crowns, adhering to a credo that he once expressed in a brief set of guidelines: "Be fair, don't bulldoze, don't bully witnesses, don't take advantage of witnesses." But it was a much larger principle that governed his conduct in the courtroom, an overriding approach to the Crown's job which he described at the end of his career. "My duty," Common said, "was not to seek a conviction, but to purely lay before the judge and jury the evidence in the Crown's possession leading to the violation of the *Criminal Code* on which the indictment was based."

He took dozens of high-profile cases. He argued the appeals in two of Ontario's most sensational murder cases, the Evelyn Dick case of the late 1940s and the Suchan-Jackson case of the early 1950s. And he appeared in constitutional cases, including those that led to the abolition of appeals to the Privy Council. But he loved to tell stories about the cases that had moments of outrageous humour, especially when the laugh was on him. That happened once at a fraud trial in Welland when Common thought he had an open-and-shut case against the accused. The jury's verdict of not guilty stunned Common. But his amazement disappeared when a spectator pointed out to him that the complainant in the case was the Imperial Bank and that two members of the jury had been put into bankruptcy by the same Imperial Bank. Common couldn't help laughing, and he repeated the story for years afterwards.

It was Common who chaired the Joint Committee on Legal Aid, which introduced the comprehensive legal aid plan to Ontario in 1966. It was Common who was the first member of the Attorney General's Office to win election as a bencher. It was Common who, after his retirement from the post of deputy attorney general in 1964, accepted a key position with James McRuer's Law Reform Commission. And it was Common who filled the role of clerk of the Ontario Legislature in the late 1960s and early 1970s. He was the man who took 10,000 cases to court, and to the end of his days he just could not stop working in jobs that served his profession and his province.

Joseph Sedgwick (1898–1981)

Joe Sedgwick wore bow ties. He drank Teacher's Scotch with a splash of Apollinaris. He played bridge and read Chesterton. He revered the British monarchy and the Anglican Church.

Joseph Sedgwick (r.) with John Arnup (l.)

He relished conversation of all kinds in the manner of a real-life version of Casper Gutman in Dashiell Hammett's *Maltese Falcon* – the character remembered for declaring, "I'm a man who likes talking to a man that likes to talk."

Sedgwick's voice had a distinctive rumble: rolling, mellifluous, and merry. No one projected a sound quite like Sedgwick's plummy *basso profundo*. As for the content of his talk when he rose in defence of a client in a courtroom, that was unpredictable. "I relied mainly on my native wit in court," he said. Sedgwick's native wit could usually be counted on to trump another counsel's studied intellectuality.

Born in Yorkshire, he came to Canada as a child, and he was still a child, just sixteen years old, when he joined the 164th Battalion of the Canadian Infantry and went overseas in the First World War. He received his call to the bar in 1923 and spent a few years in general practice before he joined the Ontario Attorney General's Office. He handled much of the AG's work in the Court of Appeal, where he found an instant comfort level that set him on a lifetime in the courts. He was also adept at a variety of off-beat tasks, joining with David Croll, the provincial minister of municipal affairs in the 1930s, in drawing *The Dionne Quintuplets Protection Act* and negotiating movie rights and commercial deals for the five little girls. "We made them a million bucks," Sedgwick said. "Without us, they would have been robbed blind."

In 1938 he embarked on his sparkling career as an all-round advocate whom clients of celebrity status sought out. He successfully defended the business tycoon Jack Kent Cooke and the Ottawa mayor Charlotte Whitton on charges of criminal libel brought by the Province of Alberta. He guided Sir Frederick Banting through his divorce proceedings in a

period when divorce was no simple matter. He sued Prime Minister Pierre Trudeau on behalf of Steve Roman, the head of Denison Mines, who was mad at the federal government for blocking the sale of a uranium company. And he defended Viola MacMillan, the queen of the stock market, on charges of benefiting from an illegal windfall.

But of all his varied cases, the one in which Sedgwick took most pride was his 1946 defence of an alleged spy. The accused man was Eric Adams, a middle-level Ottawa civil servant who was said to be a member of a ring that was passing secret government documents to the Soviets. The principal witness against Adams was Kathleen Willsher, a deputy registrar in the office of the British high commissioner. Willsher pleaded guilty to violations of the *Official Secrets Act* and testified that she had delivered documents to Adams and met with other Canadian spies at the Adams house. Testifying on his own behalf, guided by Sedgwick's deft questions, Adams said Willsher was mistaken; the so-called secret documents were routine government papers, and the meetings at the Adams house were merely intellectual gatherings of leftist theorists.

John Cartwright, the special prosecutor at the trial and later chief justice of the Supreme Court of Canada, made a strong case for Adams' guilt in his jury address. The presiding judge, Chief Justice James McRuer, echoed Cartwright's view in his own jury instructions. Sedgwick, appalled at the one-sided instructions, asked McRuer to recall the jury and put to them Sedgwick's case for the defence. McRuer did so, and the jury, with the defence arguments fresh in their minds, brought in a verdict of not guilty.

A few hours later, in a chance encounter, McRuer congratulated Sedgwick. "May I say I am grateful to you," Sedgwick replied. McRuer asked why. "M'lord," Sedgwick said, "I believe that if you had left things alone after Jack Cartwright sat down, my man would have undoubtedly been convicted."

It was a story that Sedgwick, the man who loved to talk, included among his bag of glorious tales to the end of his days.

Vera Lillian Parsons (1889–1973)

Vera Parsons worried whether she could handle the case that arrived in her office in 1944. The client, a man named Allan Baldwin, was charged with murder. Parsons had never taken a murder trial in front of a jury.

Neither had any other Ontario counsel of her sex. Parsons would be the first. Back in 1925 she had been the first woman to argue before a jury in a civil action. The case developed out of an automobile accident, and Parsons represented the plaintiff. She won at trial. But she felt doubts about defending in the Baldwin murder trial. Her first inclination was to find another counsel, a man, to lift the responsibility from her shoulders. She pondered the problem.

When Parsons had entered Osgoode Hall Law School more than a quarter century earlier, she brought with her an extensive and varied education. The daughter of a well-to-do executive at the Robert Simpson Company, she earned a Bachelor of Arts in modern languages at the University of Toronto, then a Master's in comparative literature from Bryn Mawr College near Philadelphia. She made herself fluent in Italian and studied briefly at the University of Rome, before returning home to seek a career for herself.

Her first position was with a Toronto settlement for Italian immigrants. Parsons had a kind nature, and her generosity, together with her ease in the immigrants' language, made her indispensable in helping them over the difficulties that their new country presented. Then a crisis emerged which showed Parsons her limi-

Parsons had a well-earned reputation for thoroughness in preparation and doggedness in cross-examination. She applied both qualities to the Baldwin case.

tations. A young Italian woman who was a member of the settlement got herself lost in the city. The police charged her with vagrancy. Parsons pointed out that the woman was guilty only of mistaking her way in unfamiliar surroundings. But the incident impressed on Parsons the hard truth that she could better help people like the lost Italian if she had a lawyer's training.

At Osgoode, she won the silver medal in the year of her call, 1924. She articled with a small firm headed by William Horkins, who ran a thriving criminal practice. Parsons remained with the firm after her articles, eventually becoming a partner and practising for almost fifty years. As a teenager, she had suffered from polio and needed a cane to get around. If her weakened legs seemed a handicap, it wasn't one that Parsons allowed to interfere with her work or her pleasures. She was a gifted pianist, collected art, and spent most of her free time in the summers roughing it at her cottage on Lake Temagami.

Parsons was strong-minded and independent, but the Allan Baldwin murder case daunted her. The victim of the killing was a guard at the Don Jail, where Baldwin, a convicted bank robber, was a prisoner. In an escape attempt, Baldwin assaulted the guard with his fists, then tied him up. The guard died of asphyxia, and the murder charge was brought against Baldwin. When Parsons couldn't persuade other counsel to take the case, she assumed responsibility for what seemed to everyone an open-and-shut case against her client.

Parsons had a well-earned reputation for thoroughness in preparation and doggedness in cross-examination. She applied both qualities to the Baldwin case. She gave herself a crash course in anatomy and, at the trial, she put the Crown's medical witnesses through a severe grilling. Her point was that, in the circumstances of the jail guard's death, other causes than Baldwin's actions could have brought about the asphyxiation. Under Parsons' informed questioning, the medical witnesses admitted that her arguments had a sound basis.

At the end of a first trial, the jury was unable to reach a verdict. Parsons gained confidence from the mistrial and, at the retrial, the jury decided that Baldwin was guilty only of manslaughter. This result represented a personal triumph in Parsons' admirable career at the bar and a milestone for all of Ontario's female counsel.

Margaret Paton Hyndman (1901–1991)

In 1911, when Margaret Hyndman was ten years old, her parents took her from their home in Palmerston, Ontario, to visit the House of Commons in Ottawa.

As each of the members rose to speak in the House – Laurier, Borden, and the others – Margaret's father whispered to her the speaker's profession. It seemed to the young girl that the most impressive orators were lawyers, and, from that moment, Margaret decided that she, too, would become a lawyer.

The path into the profession turned out to be strewn with obstacles and rebuffs. Since the Hyndmans couldn't afford to send their daughter to university, Margaret took the more challenging matriculant route. The lawyer for whom she articled, F.W. Wegenast of Toronto, expected her, as a mere female, to contribute secretarial duties to the firm in return for her legal training. On the day of her call in 1925, Mr. Justice Logie gave a speech welcoming the new lawyers to the bar; Logie added, referring to Hyndman and the other two women of the class, that he found it "constitutionally impossible" – meaning his own constitution made it impossible – to include the women in his welcome because there was "no room at the bar for them." When she joined the small Wegenast firm as a lawyer, her senior took it for granted that she would devote every evening over the following six years to assisting him on his ambitious study, *Wegenast on Canadian Companies*, which was at last published in 1931.

None of the insults or hurdles daunted Hyndman. She had a remarkably sunny nature and a sense of humour that never failed to carry her through the rough patches. Her intellect was strong and her determination remained unbeatable.

In 1937, working on a probate, she discovered that most of the estate consisted of shares in a Detroit brewery that had lost its management. Hyndman commuted to Detroit and kept the brewery afloat herself until she could sell the stock at a reasonable price. Nothing fazed her.

She came relatively late to her career in litigation, but once she found her own formidable style in the courtroom, she argued in a series of significant cases that touched on causes she championed. In the late 1930s, when a Toronto woman was charged with an offence for offering advice on birth control, Hyndman based her defence on an argument that the woman was acting for the public good. She won an acquittal.

Hyndman placed herself at the centre of the flap over margarine in the late 1940s and, in the process, she made a piece of legal history. A section of the *Canadian Dairy Act* forbade the sale of margarine. The federal government referred the matter to the Supreme Court of Canada, asking if it was within the government's authority to repeal the margarine section. Hyndman, representing a coalition of women's organizations, argued for the affirmative and was successful. When the government appealed the court's decision to the Privy Council, Hyndman travelled to London and became the first and only Canadian lawyer of her sex to appear before that august body. The Privy Council also held in favour of her side.

Even in her seventies, Hyndman continued to argue worthy issues in the highest courts. In 1974 she appeared in the Supreme Court on the controversial Gage case. At issue was legislation that refused the right of an Indian woman who married a white man to be registered under the *Indian Act*. Hyndman was eloquent in opposing the legislation, and, though the court held against her, the division was 5–4 and included a ringing Bora Laskin dissent.

Hyndman devoted much of her life to crusades, most frequently for the rights of women. She spoke for Canadian women in the courts. She took roles in all the country's important women's organizations. And she led by example. She was the first Canadian woman to sit on the board of a trust company, and, when she received a KC in 1938, she was the second woman in the British Commonwealth to gain the honour. Hyndman was a feminist before her time, a woman who set out to blaze new trails from the day when she was a youngster sitting in the gallery at the House of Commons.

Ernest Cecil Facer (1905–1963)

Cec Facer was a daredevil in the old-fashioned sense, the kind who accepted risk as an everyday part of his job.

When Facer practised law as a young fellow in Sudbury in the 1930s, he earned a pilot's licence and bought a fragile but frisky single-engine plane. He equipped the plane with skis for winter and floats for summer, and in every season of the year, in all weather, landing on water or snow, he flew his legal services to remote communities far beyond Sudbury. He took off for Chapleau, and northwest to Wawa, and down south to Gore Bay. Some people thought Facer was asking for trouble, but young Cec felt exhilarated up in the sky. And, besides, it was part of his practice – the counsel who flew his courtroom skills to clients out of reach of conventional consultation. There was nothing conventional about Cec Facer when he climbed behind the controls of his dauntless little plane.

Facer wasn't a Sudbury native. He grew up in Belleville, Ontario, the son of a machinist, and he articled in the office of a Belleville lawyer. But when he was called to the bar in 1929, he found no openings in his hometown. Partly by default, he turned to the north for a job in partnership with a man named R.R. McKessock, who, among other roles, held the post of Sudbury's Crown attorney. Facer threw himself into the Crown's work, but after McKessock's unexpected death within a year of Facer's arrival, he formed his own Sudbury law firm. It was a firm so rooted in the community that, passing through many changes in name and personnel, it carried on into the twenty-first century.

Facer took enthusiastically to Sudbury. He married a local woman and turned himself into the city's number one booster. He served as an alderman in the 1930s and as a charter member and governor of Laurentian University in the 1960s. In between, in his heyday, he put together a reputation as Sudbury's most respected lawyer.

In the courtroom, Facer's strength was based on traditional virtues. He knew his law, but judges, juries, and other counsel came to hold him in high regard for his probity and courtesy. The qualities were innate in Facer, a man without guile, and all the clients he appeared for in court, on both civil and criminal matters, began with the head start of a counsel whose integrity the court never questioned. "A lawyer's lawyer," was how his colleagues in town spoke of Cec Facer.

Given such respect, when a part-time job as the Sudbury District's first Juvenile Court judge opened up in 1945, it was not surprising that Facer received the appointment. What turned out to be very surprising was that Judge Facer soon made headlines across the country. He ruled that the police in his jurisdiction could no longer follow the old custom of holding juveniles in the local jail after their arrest. Such incarceration, Facer said, would only place the kids under the negative influence of adult criminals. The ruling seemed to make ordinary common sense, but no one in authority in Canada had ever before enunciated such a stand. Then Facer's view became the norm throughout the country. In recognition of this and other contributions during his eighteen years on the Juvenile Court, the new institution for young offenders which opened in Sudbury seven years after Facer's sudden death in 1964 was named the Cecil Facer Juvenile Facility.

At the time of his death, Facer was scheduled to represent the central figure in a judicial hearing into a possible political scandal in the Sudbury area, once again putting his integrity in the service of a client. But in the preceding decade, he had concentrated mostly on a solicitor's work, and it wasn't hard to understand why his favourite client was the local Austin Airlines. It was an outfit that included bush pilots among its employees, men who were Cec Facer's kind of daredevils.

Roydon Ambrose Hughes (1905–1992)

Roydon Hughes refused to describe himself as a mere trial lawyer. "I'm a trial horse," he liked to say. He accepted every case that came his way, especially criminal defences.

He loved the courtroom, couldn't stay out of it, and took cases back to back to back. Hughes learned about dedication and determination the hard way. He was the second child in an Ottawa family of twelve boys and girls and, when both parents died young, Hughes took much of the responsibility for his siblings. He received his call to the bar in 1929, the year of the stock market crash, and, partly by default, he slid into criminal work. He reasoned that the Depression eliminated most chances of making money from real estate or corporate-commercial files, but clients faced with criminal charges could usually come up with a few dollars to stay out of jail. Hughes made himself a very active member of Ottawa's criminal bar.

He cut his teeth on bootlegging cases. Since such cases invariably involved the smuggling of booze into the Prohibition-era United States, Hughes became an expert on the *Customs Act*. He mastered the intricacies in defending charges of bribing customs officers, false billing freight cars of liquor, and cooking up phony certificates of alcohol analysis. Until the end of Prohibition in late 1933, the very young Hughes was Ottawa's go-to counsel among local bootleggers.

He moved on to an eccentric and challenging series of murder cases. In one, a jeweller named Edelson was charged with shooting to death another jeweller named Horowitz. It happened that Horowitz had been having an affair with Edelson's wife. Hughes argued in Edelson's defence that his client waved the gun at Horowitz only to warn him away

from Mrs. Edelson. When Horowitz panicked and grabbed for the gun, it discharged accidentally, with tragic results. The jury, accepting the Hughes version, brought in a verdict of not guilty.

In another case, a Toronto woman named Sullivan was alleged to have killed her husband by smacking him on the head with a liquor bottle in the bathroom of their room at the Château Laurier. What gave the case a special sensitivity was the deceased Sullivan's occupation: he was a lawyer in the provincial Attorney General's Office. For the accused, Hughes marshalled an argument, based on expert medical evidence, that Sullivan suffered a spontaneous hemorrhage, striking his head on the bathtub as he fell. Again, the jury acquitted.

"You have to be an actor with juries," Hughes said, "because they watch the defence lawyer as closely as they watch the accused." The style that Hughes presented was of the calm, cool, and collected counsel. He said his manner came as a reaction to older barristers of the day who favoured a much more histrionic approach in the courtroom. That wasn't for Hughes. As he pointed out, his style was free of the emotional delivery of more senior counsel. He maintained in court a restrained and steady presence, an actor who knew how to coax the audience in the jury box.

In later years, particularly as he built the Hughes, Laishley firm, Hughes cut back his criminal work in favour of a practice in civil litigation. But the variety of his criminal defences most identified his overall career. He represented three men who were charged with espionage offences as a result of the 1945 revelations by Igor Gouzenko, the cipher clerk at the Soviet Embassy, of a Communist spy network in Canada. Of Hughes' three clients, two were acquitted and one was convicted, receiving a three-year sentence.

In yet another memorable Hughes case, he was the personal choice of the great criminal lawyer Arthur Maloney to defend Maloney's brother-in-law on a charge of robbing a store in Cornwall, Ontario. Hughes mounted a defence based on identification. In cross-examinations of the Crown witnesses, he established that the police had displayed a photograph of the accused to the witnesses of the robbery before they picked out his client at an identification lineup. The brother-in-law was acquitted. Arthur Maloney knew he had chosen the right defence lawyer: he knew that Roydon Hughes was a horse for trial work.

Mayer Lerner (1906–2000)

Mayer Lerner's own version of his life story was that he set out in the law as a very reluctant student. It was his father, a Russian-born merchant in London, Ontario, who decreed that young Mayer would attend Osgoode Hall Law School.

The son had other ideas: he wanted to be a stockbroker, and he spent a summer in Manhattan in the mid-1920s learning his way around the New York Stock Exchange. But, obeying his dad, he enrolled at Osgoode where, according to him, he skipped classes and set a record for the number of supplemental exams he wrote. He had money troubles too; he arrived in first year with $2,000, which he had saved to cover expenses during his entire Osgoode career, but promptly lost the whole stake in bad investments. Ever resourceful, for replacement income he wangled a part-time reporting job at the *Toronto Star* covering inquests, which happened, fortuitously, to be held in the evenings in those days.

Called to the bar in 1929, Lerner opened a one-man practice back home in London. His first clients were a pair of recidivist chicken thieves charged with another crime in their specialty. With Lerner defending, the two were convicted once again, but Lerner collected a fee of $8, which he liked, and he discovered that he felt at ease in the courtroom, which he liked even more. He knew he possessed a fierce streak of competitiveness, and a counsel's work struck him as the right outlet for a man who revelled in a battle.

He concentrated on criminal cases in his early years, serving for a time as an assistant Crown attorney, then building a reputation as the sharpest defence counsel in southwestern Ontario. His fame spread with his thrilling defence of a

man facing the gallows in the murder of his wife's lover. Though the case against his client seemed irrefutable, Lerner's ingeniously constructed argument of provocation convinced the jury, which brought in a manslaughter verdict.

When Lerner's younger brother Sam joined him in the 1940s, the two men built a practice that grew into the largest firm in Ontario outside Toronto and Ottawa. During this period of extraordinary expansion, Mayer Lerner turned principally to civil litigation of an immense variety. He was especially relentless in preparation, compiling over the years two black-leather loose-leaf notebooks covering a vast array of points of law. The distinctive notebooks were his constant companions, and he knew he was on to a good thing when judges asked, somewhat sheepishly, to borrow the invaluable books.

In his litigation practice, Lerner backed down from no man. When he acted for a group of unfortunate Tilsonburg farmers who had been flimflammed out of their land in the 1960s by a powerful Texas family, he was warned that, if he ventured into the Texans' home territory to take discoveries, not even the FBI could guarantee his safety. Lerner headed south anyway, and in a characteristic display of bravado and smarts he forced the Texas family to capitulate by threatening to put the Canadian tax authorities on it for profiting in the Tilsonburg land. The Ontario farmers got back their properties.

In 1971 the minister of justice, John Turner, asked Lerner if he would accept an appointment to the bench. "My people have canvassed scores of lawyers about you," Turner said. "Half say they worship you, and the other half say they can't stand you. There doesn't seem to be anybody you haven't made an impression on." Lerner loved the story, and equally loved his years as a judge.

In his late seventies, retired from the bench, he worked as a pre-trial mediator. In his eighties, he sat on a review panel reporting to the provincial College of Physicians and Surgeons. For a man who claimed he started out as a reluctant Osgoode Hall student, Mayer Lerner forged a remarkably enduring and triumphant record in the law.

John Josiah Robinette (1906–1996)

At the time John J. Robinette accepted the Evelyn Dick case in late 1946, he was already well known among his fellow members of the litigation bar.

They were aware that he had graduated from Osgoode Hall Law School in 1929 with the gold medal, that he had returned to the school as a precise and orderly lecturer, that he had edited the *Ontario Law Reports*, and that he had developed a courtroom practice at both trial and appeal as "a pretty good technical lawyer" – as he modestly described himself. Then the Dick case came along, altering for a short time the trajectory of his career and extending for all time the reach of his fame.

Evelyn Dick was a courtesan to the gentry in Hamilton, Ontario. When the torso of her husband's body turned up on Hamilton Mountain, the police charged her with her husband's murder. A jury convicted Mrs. Dick at a first trial. She hired Robinette to appeal the conviction. He succeeded on the appeal, and, at the second trial, his careful cross-examination discredited the Crown's key witness and was instrumental in winning an acquittal.

The Dick case attracted media attention of unprecedented intensity. In the process, it made Robinette a household name. Not even his full name was necessary to identify him to the man on the street: the initials were enough. According to public opinion, "JJ" was the greatest lawyer in the land. Public opinion was correct, though Robinette wasn't happy with the layperson's concept of him as exclusively a criminal lawyer. He thought of himself, correctly, as a generalist of the courtroom.

Nevertheless, in the decade after the Dick trial, he accepted nearly a score more capital cases, mainly because he could never say no to anyone, least of all to a poor soul facing a murder charge. Just one of his capital cases resulted in the ultimate penalty: Steve Suchan, convicted in the autumn of 1952 in the shooting of a Toronto police detective, was hanged at the Don Jail. It was a fate that profoundly shook the gentle Robinette.

By the late 1950s he had put most criminal work behind him in favour of civil cases, which he found more varied and intricate. Constitutional disputes, legislative interpretations, combines prosecutions, a high-profile libel action involving Toronto's mayor Allan Lamport, the trial over millions of dollars in gold rights which pitted him against his colleague John Arnup and endured for more than a year and a half – Robinette was a wonder of versatility. He loved legal research, something that he, the ultimate loner, handled himself for each of his cases. He needed no juniors, though he sometimes took one to court for the companionship. Robinette may have been shy, but he made wonderful company. It was his sense of humour that helped him in carrying the ferocious volume of work he performed in the nation's courtrooms.

He possessed the physical tools of the superior counsel: attractive face, robust build, resonant baritone voice. He was sublime at taking the measure of judges and juries. He seemed to know intuitively what they would buy, and, conversely, particularly in appeal courts, he had a talent for setting the courtroom agenda, for telling the judges what arguments were, in effect, available for purchase. While he was a model of courtesy in court, he wasn't above shaking his head in amazed doubt during an opposing counsel's argument, sending a signal to the bench of his own views. Not surprisingly, most judges found themselves receptive to the signal.

He preached his versions of the three Cs of advocacy: chronology, candour, and clarity. He insisted on correct punctuation and grammar. He argued from scripted notes in appeal. His spoken language was the same as his written language: simple and direct. He urged others, as himself, to be ever succinct.

His durability made him a phenomenon. At seventy-four, he led the 1981 argument in the Supreme Court of Canada in the country's most historically significant constitutional case. At seventy-six, he defended in a five-week political corruption trial in Nova Scotia. To the end of his honourable career, which spanned more than half a century, he remained the foremost counsel of his era.

In 1965 John Robinette became the first president of The Advocates' Society.

Francis Andrew Brewin (1907–1983)

Andy Brewin had more than enough stick-to-it-iveness for a dozen men. As a CCF candidate, then as an NDPer, he ran for office six times, beginning in 1945, once provincially and the rest federally.

He lost in every single election. He ran again in 1962 in the federal riding of Toronto Greenwood and, this time, he won. He got himself re-elected in six more campaigns and sat in the House of Commons for seventeen years, serving with distinction as his party's defence and external affairs critic. Brewin hadn't allowed the string of losses at the beginning of his political career to deter him from the path he was determined to follow. He had single-mindedness of an unstoppable order.

He brought the same quality to his work in litigation. Where other counsel might see a certain loser of a case, he spotted an opportunity to try a new argument or a different approach to an old point. He was beaten in his share of cases, but defeat never came from a lack of effort or ingenuity. His powers of concentration made him a legend among his colleagues. They also made him a sometimes absent-minded husband, often forgetting to take care of the household accounts. On one occasion his wife, Peggy, called the office asking a Brewin partner to beg her husband to pay the telephone bill. Peggy was calling from a phone booth because Bell had cut off its services.

Brewin grew up the son of an Anglican clergyman – his father was rector at Toronto's St. Simon the Apostle for nineteen years – and the lessons of Christian compassion stayed with him all his life. Called to the bar in 1930, he worked for the next decade as junior to James McRuer, who conducted a wide-ranging litigation practice until his appointment to the bench in 1944. Above all, in his patient apprenticeship, Brewin learned the lesson of clarity. As he began to build his own client base, Brewin's courtroom arguments were notable for their persuasive logic. He was a stickler for simplicity and steered clear of histrionics.

To the chagrin of McRuer, a dedicated Liberal, Brewin joined the new CCF Party in 1935. He said he was intellectually converted to socialism by George Bernard Shaw's *Intelligent Woman's Guide to Socialism* and spiritually converted by his conclusion that the CCF's founding members stood for principles much closer than other brands of politics to the Christian tradition. Years later, McRuer wrote that Brewin would have been one of the greatest of all Canadian counsel if he hadn't devoted himself with such fervour to politics.

Even so, Brewin left a lasting mark in the courtroom. Inevitably, his clients mirrored his political commitment in a practice that leaned to labour law and immigration issues. He favoured appeal work over trial appearances, and he argued regularly in the Supreme Court of Canada and twice before the Privy Council. In the first of the two latter cases he opposed the 1945 plan of the federal government to deport all Japanese Canadian citizens, and in the second he defended the Saskatchewan *Trade Labour Act*, an advanced piece of legislation that Brewin had helped to draft.

His last trip to the Supreme Court came in 1963, a year after his election to the House of Commons. His client was Moses MacKay, a union official who had run unsuccessfully for the federal NDP in the Toronto suburb of Etobicoke two elections earlier. During the campaign, MacKay put up the usual signs promoting his candidacy. Etobicoke made him take them down, citing a local bylaw prohibiting such signs on private property. Brewin argued that the bylaw was beyond the authority of the municipality, and the court agreed. It was a victory that ended Brewin's first career as a litigator and arrived at the beginning of his second career as an elected representative. Both careers perfectly reflected the causes he championed so passionately.

Edson Livingston Haines
(1906–1996)

Although the adult Edson Haines's erect bearing, immaculate suits, and silvery hair gave him the appearance of an aristocrat, he grew up as the son of a millright in Hamilton, Ontario.

By age twelve, he formed the notion of becoming a lawyer, but, since his family lacked the resources for him to attend university, he took the matriculant route into the profession. From high school he went to work as an articling student in the office of a Hamilton criminal lawyer named M.J. O'Reilly, who assigned simple cases in Police Court to the teenager. Haines got the idea he might practise criminal law himself one day.

He changed his mind when he moved to Toronto to take classes at Osgoode Hall and to article with Thomas Phelan, a prominent civil litigator. Phelan's practice concentrated on motor vehicle cases, acting for the cream of the insurance companies. Haines fell in love with the work. "I was bitten by the litigation bug," he explained.

On his call to the bar in 1930, Haines joined his senior as a fellow lawyer and, in no time at all, he learned the intricacies of automobile cases, acting for the Phelan list of insurer clients. He became so expert at it that, three years later, in 1933, he set himself up in his own practice. In the following years, Haines was joined by his brother, Doug, and by Jim Thomson and Bill Rogers in what was to become one of Bay Street's most formidable firms.

(Left to Right) Paul Haines, Vera Haines, Edson Haines, Barbara Haines, and Bruce Haines

Early on, in the 1930s, Haines developed what he considered to be an infallible system for settling lawsuits at the discovery stage. First came painstaking preparation. "The basic idea was to give the plaintiff second thoughts," Haines said. He hired the most thorough investigators to look into the accident's circumstances, and the top physicians in each branch of medicine to examine the plaintiff's injuries. Then came discovery.

Haines recognized that liability and special damages were rarely an issue. It was the general damages, the plaintiff's injury or disability, that became the point of contention. As soon as discovery was completed, Haines took the plaintiff's lawyer aside and spent an hour arriving at a settlement. Nine times out of ten, the sum agreed on was the number Haines had first suggested. He had an innate feel for such cases and, before he and the plaintiff's lawyer left the discovery, Haines had written a cheque for the final number. "I settled fast and quick," he said of his system.

He possessed all the qualities of a skilled and supremely confident counsel. He was an eloquent and persuasive talker; it turned out to be no coincidence that his parents had named him Edson after a famous New York City orator of the early twentieth century. And he worked indefatigably to master the medical nuances of trauma and physical damages. It was Haines, with this large store of accumulated knowledge, who led the way in forming the Medico-Legal Society in 1952.

His compassionate side was reflected in a particularly troubling 1940s case. A young girl, injured in an auto accident, suffered a disability that was certain to worsen with the years. Haines set up an arrangement that guaranteed the girl lifetime help in the same manner as an annuity. The result made him the first Ontario lawyer to put together a structured settlement.

Haines was generous in spreading his wisdom and the tricks of his trade. For thirteen years he taught a course in civil trial procedure for two hours each Saturday morning at the University of Toronto Law School. He became one of the first Canadian members of the American Trial Lawyers' Association, and he joined the International Academy of Trial Lawyers.

In 1962, when he accepted an appointment to the Ontario High Court, he continued to be an innovator, particularly noted for his skill and firm guidance in pre-trial conferences with counsel. On the bench, as in his practice, Haines was the man who brought efficiency and speed to every enterprise he embarked on.

Bernard Cohn (1908–1982)

Barney Cohn always got his hair trimmed by a barber named Jacobs who had a shop in Windsor's Prince Edward Hotel. One day in 1954, Jacobs told Cohn that his nephew desperately needed a top lawyer.

The nephew, a loudmouth named Donald Ritchie, had bragged to a newspaper reporter that he had been present six years earlier during the shocking attempt in Detroit to assassinate Walter Reuther, the head of the United Auto Workers. Reading of Ritchie's boast, the Michigan cops arrested him in Windsor and stashed him at Detroit's Brook Cadillac Hotel. Ritchie escaped back to Windsor, and now the State of Michigan was initiating extradition proceedings. Cohn assured Jacobs that he would take Ritchie's case.

Michigan retained a Windsor Crown attorney named Bruce McDonald to handle the extradition. McDonald's nickname, the Bulldog, was a tribute to his tenacity, but, at the hearing, Cohn's creative cross-examination of McDonald's key witnesses, two Detroit police detectives, so destroyed the case against Ritchie that the Bulldog threw in the towel. McDonald conceded that the application for extradition would have to be dismissed. The hearing, which was the stuff of front-page headlines in Windsor, cemented Cohn's already acknowledged reputation as the dean of the city's criminal bar.

A native of Windsor, Cohn was called to the bar in 1931. He set up a one-man practice in his hometown, to which he devoted the next fifty-two years of his life. He argued at least three dozen murder cases over the course of his career, never losing a client to the gallows or to a first-degree conviction. Other counsel thought it was Cohn's gifts as a scholar that

(Left to Right) Bernard Cohn QC, Rt. Hon. Bora Laskin, PC, QC, Hon. G. Arthur Martin, OC, QC

accounted for his success in the courts; the word around town was that Barney read the Canadian *Criminal Code* cover to cover once a day. It was true that nobody was sharper than Cohn at picking up an error in an indictment or ferreting out a fatal mistake in the Crown's case, but he contended that he always won his cases on the facts.

He also insisted that the right attitude to his clients played a big part in reaching a positive result in the courtroom. "A good criminal lawyer has to know his client personally," Cohn said. "There can't be an aloofness, whether you like the guy or not. You can't treat them like machines."

Cohn's long list of admirers included the province's most accomplished criminal lawyers of the day. "Next to Arthur Martin," Charles Dubin said, "Barney knows more criminal law than anyone in Canada." Martin was a Cohn fan from the day in 1945 when Cohn conferred with the younger Martin on a criminal appeal. "Barney," Martin said later, "is a great humanist, free from bigotry or prejudice, a man of both worldliness and an understanding of the common man."

Martin appreciated Cohn as a raconteur, a spinner of tales from the courtroom, and both men shared an unquench-able enthusiasm for racehorses. Cohn was seldom seen in his Windsor hangouts without a copy of the *Detroit Free Press* folded open to the racing page. He was also seldom spotted without a cigar clenched between his teeth. Cohn shared a small office with a commercial lawyer named David Richardson, who was another cigar devotee. The two men generated so many fumes that their favourite secretary handed in her notice. Cohn was pained to see the woman leave, but he would have been even more distressed to give up his beloved cigars.

Cohn contributed unselfishly to his profession. He was a president of the Essex County Law Association, and, when the revamped legal aid program came into effect in Ontario in 1966, it was Cohn who took the lead in implementing the system in the Windsor area. He served as a bencher, and became a life member of the Law Society in 1981. He died the following year, but his name and talent continue to be celebrated in the Bernard Cohn Memorial Lectures, an annual forum at the University of Windsor featuring the kind of criminal law that Barney Cohn practised with such genius and compassion.

Brendan O'Brien (b. 1909)

Even in cases that Brendan O'Brien lost in court, he received unexpected rewards. That was what happened in an appeal he took for a woman who sued a Toronto surgeon, claiming he had bungled an operation on her back which left her in permanent agony.

The woman, with another counsel, lost at trial, and O'Brien was retained to argue before the Court of Appeal. O'Brien thought he presented a strong case, but the appellate court dismissed the appeal. Despite the result, O'Brien's client told him she recognized how magnificently he had argued the case. Then she demonstrated her gratitude. "It was the only case I ever had where my client kissed me," O'Brien said later.

O'Brien deserved hundreds more kisses – or at least firm handshakes – in the course of his extraordinarily prolific career in which he consistently gave the best account of himself. Called to the bar in 1932, he was still conducting cases more than sixty years later, when he had entered the ninth decade of his life. He was first, last, and always an advocate, and he spread the net wide in his advocacy, taking cases of enormous variety. He often said that he thought of himself as a general counsel, in the same manner as doctors were general practitioners.

He served his articles with Phelan & Richardson and remained with the firm under its various names for the rest of his career. In the early years, he handled the cases for insurers that the Phelan practice was noted for. But over the decades, O'Brien broadened his range dramatically. He acted for clients as diverse as the CBC and the Law Society of Upper Canada. He argued the first case that came before the Supreme Court of Canada under the *Charter of Rights*. In a case involving the CPR, he helped to establish a precedent for the rights of preferred shareholders. And it was his argument

in court that led to a change in the phrase printed on Canadian currency. No longer was "Pay to bearer on demand" sufficient. Henceforth, as the inevitable result of O'Brien's advocacy, the phrase became "This note is legal tender."

He was an advocate who remained ever on the alert for ways to improve his skills. "A lot of what you learn in a counsel's work," he said, "is in waiting for your own case to be called and listening to how the case ahead of you is argued." O'Brien was the perfect observer. He came of age when the last of the grand old counsel were still practising, and, in court, he studied the styles of W.N. Tilley ("like a sledgehammer"), D.L. McCarthy ("a vast array of knowledge"), and Charlie Bell ("a counsel who used charm"). O'Brien absorbed the varying approaches and arrived at his own individual courtroom persona. He was the counsel who projected courtesy, control, and preparedness. Ontario's courtrooms never saw the day when Brendan O'Brien was caught short on a point of law or a misplaced fact.

He loved jury work. "Any bad results I ever came across in jury cases," he said, "resulted either from inept counsel or inept judges, more likely the latter." And he was equally at home in appeal. "You always got a good hearing in the Supreme Court of Canada," he said, "and sometimes a little entertainment too." O'Brien was hugely entertained on the day he argued an auto accident case before the Supreme Court. A pedestrian crossing a downtown Toronto street in the middle of the block had been struck by a car backing into a parking space. At trial, the judge apportioned the fault fifty-fifty. The Court of Appeal changed the fault to ninety-ten against O'Brien's client, the motorist. As he began his argument on appeal before the Supreme Court, Mr. Justice Jean-Philippe Pigeon interrupted him to ask, "Is there no law in Toronto against jay walking?" O'Brien thought the question, which he found so entertaining, signalled a favourable view for his argument. He was right. Led by Justice Pigeon, the court ruled in O'Brien's favour, holding that the appeal court was wrong in changing the trial judge's decision on the degree of fault.

O'Brien was first at many things. He was the first Law Society treasurer of the Catholic faith since 1804. He founded the Osgoode Society and served as its first president. And, in his later career, he wrote his first book, *Speedy Justice*, an account of the complications arising from the wreck in 1804 on Lake Ontario of a ship named the *H.M.S. Speedy*. The book, an absorbing work of thorough scholarship, demonstrated that O'Brien was capable of nothing less than the finest in authorship, as in advocacy.

John Douglas Arnup (b. 1911)

In 1947 John Arnup appeared in the Supreme Court of Canada, arguing for the appellant in a real property case.

It was the first time he had taken a case on his own in the Court and, at the end of his argument, a clearly impressed Chief Justice Thibaudeau Rinfret turned to the justice on his right and whispered, "Who is this young man?"

"He used to be Kellock's junior," the justice answered, referring to Roy Kellock, another member of the court.

"Oh," Rinfret said, "that explains it."

Arnup spent a lifetime impressing judges and other counsel. He later described one of his mentors, Gershom Mason, as "intelligent and methodical, analytical, polished, and low key." That description applied equally to Arnup. He set off no fireworks in the courtroom, except those of an intellectual sort. He was uncommonly well organized, the rare counsel who often seemed able to get out of the office at 5:30 p.m. (particularly on winter Tuesdays, his inviolable night for curling). And he had a superior gift with words, a writer who laid out his arguments in phrasing that was clear to the neophyte but never insulted the veteran.

Born in Toronto, the son of a Methodist clergyman, Arnup attended Victoria College before he enrolled in Osgoode Hall Law School. There he had a peculiar experience. In the year of his call to the bar, 1935, he finished first in the class but didn't receive the gold medal. The reason was

that a lecturer at the school, the charismatic and often controversial Cecil Wright, had given him 60 per cent in agency in first year. By the rules, a mark so low disqualified Arnup from eligibility for the gold medal, no matter how astronomically high he scored in his other exams.

Arnup hardly allowed the disappointment to slow his ambition. "I wanted to do nothing but litigation," he said, "and I wanted to do it right away." He joined the firm where he had articled, Mason, Foulds, and began the process of fitting himself into its long tradition of eminent counsel. He learned by sitting at the side of Mason and Kellock. He digested their lessons in careful preparation and orderly presentation. And when his turn came, he slid seamlessly into the ranks of the stellar advocates of his generation.

If it is possible to single out one shining case in a career as diverse as Arnup's, it would be *Leitch Gold Mines v. Texas Gulf Sulphur* from the late 1960s. The epic trial pitted Arnup against his friend John Robinette, two grand counsel at the peak of their abilities. The dispute between Leitch, Robinette's client, and Texas Gulf, represented by Arnup, boiled down to a matter of contract: Did Texas Gulf agree to give Leitch a 10 per cent interest in northern Ontario lands on which a fortune in minerals was subsequently discovered? Leitch claimed that Texas Gulf owed it a half-billion dollars in damages for breach of contract. After a year of discoveries, the case went to trial before Mr. Justice George Gale, sitting without a jury.

The case involved abstruse concepts of metallurgy, geology, cartography, and much other deep science. Altogether, the trial, which included one notably crafty cross-examination by Arnup, kept the two counsel in courtroom battle for 164 days, spread over a year and a half. Robinette's fight was more uphill than Arnup's. Nevertheless, both men struggled against exhaustion, particularly in the final arguments to Gale which lasted sixteen days. Gale worked at his judgment for seven months, ending one of the great contests in Ontario courtroom history by finding in favour of Arnup's client.

In 1970 Arnup was appointed to the Court of Appeal, lending to his new tasks two qualities in particular. One was his lucid and graceful writing style, and the other was an unassailable creed, which he had adopted from the United Church: a commitment "to seek justice and to resist evil." John Arnup measured up to both promises.

Dalton Gilbert Dean (1911–1981)

In December 1945, in the German town of Aurich, Dalton Dean was assigned a key role in the most significant of all the trials he would conduct in his long and rewarding career as a counsel.

Dean, a thirty-four-year-old Canadian Army major at the time, was one of the three prosecutors in the court martial of Kurt Meyer, the commanding officer of Germany's infamous 12th SS Panzer Division. The case that Dean and his colleagues set out to prove was that Meyer directed the murder of twenty-seven Canadian soldiers who had been taken prisoner in Normandy during the weeks immediately after the D-Day invasion in June 1944. For Canada, the Meyer court martial represented the most personal and meaningful calling to account of the German enemy. Dean and the other prosecutors called twenty-nine witnesses to make the case, and the court, deliberating over several days, brought in a verdict of guilty. Meyer was sentenced to death, but the senior presiding officer, Major-General Chris Vokes, commuted the sentence to life imprisonment. Meyer would go free in 1956. Dean, meanwhile, won promotion to lieutenant-colonel in recognition of his outstanding contribution to the court martial and, on his discharge in March 1946, he returned with relief and satisfaction to his life in the law in northern Ontario.

Dean had grown up in Tilsonburg, Ontario, and attended the University of Western Ontario, where he played football and won a Rhodes Scholarship. Called to the bar in 1936, he answered a newspaper ad for a lawyer in Haileybury. The young and eager Dean moved north, married the local bank manager's daughter, and put down roots in the town. The war deflected his plans for his four years of army service, but afterwards he spent a short period as Kirkland Lake's Crown attorney. Then he bought a retired lawyer's practice in Haileybury and settled in for the long haul.

Dean handled much of the solicitor's work connected to the area's mining industry. He tended to the mines' corporate books, prepared prospectuses for companies registering on the stock exchange, drew wills for the wealthy mine

Dean defended in several murder cases, and, in all of them, he gained for his clients either an acquittal or a conviction on a lesser charge. Juries could never resist a Dean defence.

managers, and later probated their estates. But it was the courtroom that quickened his blood. Though the solicitor's fees were necessary to earn a living in the north, Dean was at heart a counsel, in both civil and criminal cases.

He stood over six feet tall and had a sonorous voice that commanded attention. Even with the advantage of this natural equipment, he chose an understated approach in the courtroom. When a judge challenged him on a point of law, Dean answered in a manner that seemed almost apologetic, as if he regretted that he understood more than the judge about the case and its law. With such an attitude, Dean was a counsel to whom judges, and juries too, couldn't help responding.

Throughout the north, he took the defence for personal injury cases on behalf of the Manitoba Public Insurance and Cooperators Insurance. As the most popular lawyer in the area, he also represented his share of plaintiffs in injury claims. A young lawyer named Ian Gordon, who worked in the Sudbury office of Greg Evans (later chief justice of Ontario), travelled Ontario's northeast doing insurance defence work, and whenever he came up against Dean, Gordon lost. Finally one morning, in the counsel room of the Haileybury Courthouse, Dean asked Gordon if he wasn't tired of the defeats. When Gordon admitted with a weary smile that the losses were becoming annoying, Dean invited Gordon to join him in a partnership that endured and prospered in Haileybury for years.

From the close vantage point of the partnership, Gordon recognized that Dean was even better than he had thought. He marvelled at Dean's commitment to his criminal clients. Dean defended in several murder cases, and, in all of them, he gained for his clients either an acquittal or a conviction on a lesser charge. Juries could never resist a Dean defence.

During his career, the modest Dean displayed no hint in his office of his service in the Meyer court martial, nor did he discuss the events of December 1945 with friends. But years after Dean's death in 1981, his granddaughter Christine went on the Internet searching out information for a school paper about her grandfather. To her surprise and delight, she found a photograph of him in the courtroom at Aurich. Her grandfather Dean was standing tall and resolute in uniform beside Kurt Meyer, the enemy whose conviction he had worked so honourably to ensure.

Gordon Fripp Henderson (1912–1993)

Gordon Henderson wasn't yet two years at the bar when he won his first triumph in the field of law that became his specialty.

Called to the bar in 1937, Henderson joined the Ottawa firm of Henderson & Herridge (the Henderson of the title was George, no relation to Gordon). Gordon Gowling was the partner who handled the firm's busy litigation practice in trade-marks, patents, and copyright, and it was he who handed young Henderson a case that Gowling considered a sure loser. The case was highly technical, concerning the refusal of the Patent Office to allow a claim for patent, and though it was Henderson & Herridge's contention for the plaintiff that the Patent Office was obliged under law to accept the claim, Gowling told young Henderson that the case was weak, no more than a chance for him to gain experience. Undeterred by Gowling's gloomy forecast, Henderson proceeded to win at trial, in both the Court of Appeal and the Supreme Court of Canada.

"From then on," Henderson said, looking back on the case years later, "I had Gordon Gowling's confidence."

He had far more than that. He had the beginning of a career that made him one of the foremost litigators in the kind of law that later became known as intellectual property. Henderson was versatile, shining in combines and tax work, and succeeding in negligence and commercial cases. But intellectual property was where he performed as a counsel of craft and diligence, perhaps rivalled in the field only by Donald Sim of Toronto.

His recipe for success was simple. Once, speaking of the challenges in appearing before the Court of Appeal in the 1940s, when the judges were notably querulous, Henderson said, "They were difficult, but if you knew your case and dealt with the legal issues properly, you enjoyed a good hearing." He spent a lifetime mastering his cases and dealing impeccably with the legal issues. He always enjoyed a good hearing.

He was a counsel with an original turn of mind. In one trial in the 1940s, he persuaded the judge to allow home movies to be screened as evidence in the courtroom. That constituted a first in a Canadian court and, in the same decade, Henderson chalked up another first when he prevailed on a judge to permit a tape recording into evidence. He won a case in which he argued that "Frigidaire" was an invalid trade-mark, and he won again in a similar argument over the invalidity of the trade-mark "Wilkinson Sword." He blazed trails in the licensing of popular songs and in the spread of cable TV. And he shared his knowledge with other lawyers by founding and editing *The Canadian Patent Reporter*, an indispensable summary of patent cases.

Fellow counsel knew Henderson as a tough opponent who was industrious with his talents. It was typical of Henderson that he went to bat for Leo Landreville, a one-time judge who was the subject of a withering report by a royal commission conducted by Mr. Justice Ivan Rand. Henderson won a ruling in court that quashed the report and gained Landreville the pension that the government was declining to pay him.

Henderson was indefatigable on behalf of Ottawa charities, he became a life bencher, and he received the Order of Canada. He taught at Carleton University and the University of Ottawa. And he served as the honorary counsel general for Liberia. He joked that he never visited Liberia itself, a trip that was virtually the only thing of personal significance that the gregarious and energetic Gordon Henderson missed out on in his entire life.

Henry Herbert Bull (1911–1968)

When Henry Bull was preparing his Crown's addresses to the jury, he rehearsed in front of a mirror. He examined each gesture, calculating its impact on the jury.

He studied his facial expressions and considered the cadence of the words he spoke. The man was meticulous in readying himself for the courtroom. He left nothing to chance.

His clothes were immaculate, his posture ramrod straight, his manners impeccable. In all ways he represented such a perfect embodiment of the Crown attorney that the National Film Board, shooting a 1964 instructional movie about the workings of legal aid in York County, asked Bull to take the role of the prosecutor. No one else could play the part so convincingly. The NFB called it type casting.

Bull's journey to the Crown's office began in Windsor, Ontario, where he was born, the son of a music teacher. Young Henry inherited his father's artistic gene, though, in the son, the expression in the arts came by way of pen and ink. He was a deft cartoonist, and, in later years, he was acclaimed for the caricatures he drew of fellow counsel and judges. He sketched while he sat in the courtroom, portraits that he once called "the bobtailed freaks of a warped imagination." But they weren't mere doodles; they were splendid miniatures of art that earned display in Toronto galleries.

After Bull's call to the bar in 1938, he worked in the Succession Duty Office for two years, then became an assistant Crown attorney. He stayed in the Crown's office for the rest of his working life, taking time away only to serve in the

Royal Regiment of Canada during the Second World War. He was a spit-and-polish soldier, solid in his duty, and when he was demobilized in 1946 it was with the rank of major.

Bull once told an interviewer that he was a neutral party in the courtroom. "The Crown never wins," he said, "and the Crown never loses." But the quote failed to tell the whole story. It was true that Bull had a compassionate side; after all, his first choice of profession, before he switched to law, lay in the Anglican ministry. Nor was he without a sense of humour, often beginning his addresses to the jury with the line, "Now, I don't want you to be impressed by my eloquence." But as the Crown's representative, Bull was most characterized by his tough and remorseless advocacy. Defence counsel couldn't expect a break from Henry Bull, and judges needed to stay on their toes.

He prosecuted murder cases in an era when those found guilty were sentenced to be hanged. Among other trials, Bull handled the 1962 prosecution of Arthur Lucas, who was charged with stabbing a man and a woman to death in a midtown Toronto rooming house. Bull contended that Lucas, who was from Detroit, as were the victims, was a hired gun carrying out a professional execution for a kingpin in Michigan drug dealing. To support his case, Bull called sixty-five witnesses, filed 105 exhibits, and presented a minutely detailed address to the jury. It was a vintage performance, one that convinced the jury to bring in a guilty verdict. On December 11, 1962, Lucas was hanged at the Don Jail back to back with another convicted murderer, Ronald Turpin (who was prosecuted by Bull's colleague, Arthur Klein). They were the last two men to be executed in Canada.

Not long after the Lucas trial, Bull was promoted to be Crown attorney for York County, a move that took him out of the courts. His new job called for his full-time administrative skills in overseeing all the deputy Crowns and in increasing their numbers. While at his desk one morning in September 1968, he suffered a heart attack that killed him in an instant. It seemed entirely fitting that Henry Bull died while he was busy with the Crown's work.

Goldwin Arthur Martin (1913–2001)

When Arthur Martin graduated from Osgoode Hall Law School in 1938 at the top of his class, his decision to practise at the criminal bar struck many senior lawyers as heretical for a gold medalist.

At the time, criminal lawyers were widely regarded as a lower form of the profession. But early in Martin's practice, he found a moral base to his choice. "I arrived in court in the mornings and found accused men held literally in a cage, begging to plead guilty to put an end to their humiliation," Martin said. "I felt a duty to help each man in the cage."

With such a philosophy, and with his consummate intellect, Martin almost single-handedly effected a change in the practice and perception of criminal law. He set an example in advocacy that brought new respectability to criminal work, and his scholarship initiated a more analytical approach to the concepts of law in the field. In his arguments at trial and on appeal, in his writings and his teaching, he pioneered fresh approaches to legal aid, bail reform, Crown disclosure of evidence, the defence of insanity, and safeguards on wiretap evidence. Over almost fifty years of service as a counsel and as a member of the Court of Appeal, Martin left his fingerprints on virtually every new idea in criminal law.

Not long after he received his call to the bar, his practice got off to a sensational start. The veteran criminal Mickey MacDonald had been convicted of murdering a bookie. Martin won a new trial with an argument that, particularly coming from a very young counsel, dazzled the Court of Appeal. At the retrial, Martin successfully defended MacDonald. Three months later, Martin again succeeded in his representation of MacDonald, this time in a robbery case. Three years further on, when MacDonald approached Martin to defend him on charges of kidnapping, Martin turned MacDonald away. To do otherwise, Martin said, was to give himself the appearance of a mouthpiece for the underworld. From then on, with occasional significant exceptions, his clients tended to be people who found themselves in their first – and usually their only – serious trouble with the law.

The underpinnings of Martin's courtroom style were built on civility, restraint, and good manners. He sat at the defence counsel's table, hands folded in his lap, his face an agreeable mask of equanimity. He looked not unlike a man waiting to help an elderly lady across the street. When he rose to question witnesses, he first apologized for detaining them and assured them he intended to be brief. He invariably was. His addresses to juries – and his arguments in appeal courts – were similarly the opposite of the scattergun attack. Martin was a master at confining his case to the one or two points that judges and juries would seize on as reasons for their decisions.

As a counsel, he possessed many advantages. A prodigious memory was one; he was able to recall in an instant relevant cases and their citations, sometimes the very number of the page in the volume on which the report began. Martin's sister Arlene, simply by her presence as his secretary and guardian of the gates, gave him another advantage: no one reached Martin, potential clients in particular, until they had been vetted by the elegant and formidable Arlene.

Since brother and sister remained single and lived together, Arlene ordered parts of Martin's domestic life as microscopically as his office life. She shared his great affection for horse racing. Martin loved to visit Woodbine's backstretch early in the morning to watch the horses work out. He loved racing even more when Scarlett O'Hara, a horse from his own small stable, won a stakes race.

When he received his appointment to the Court of Appeal in 1973, Martin, a man of enormous rectitude, gave up horses because he thought it would be unseemly for a justice to frequent a place of gambling. On the bench, his decisions in criminal appeals set a high standard in insight and precedent, and, on the day he retired, one of his court colleagues said, "Now that Arthur's gone, the rest of us will have to start learning the *Criminal Code*." The colleague was only half kidding.

John Thomas Weir (1912–1976)

One morning in the mid-1950s, Jack Weir appeared before Justice Fred Barlow in Weekly Court seeking relief by way of mandamus. Mandamus was all the rage at the time, though not with Justice Barlow.

Ten other mandamus applications came before him that morning, and he dismissed each of them. When Weir rose to make his pitch on the eleventh, Barlow asked him why it should be treated any differently from the previous ten.

"Well, your Lordship," Weir answered, "I've always thought it more important to be right than consistent."

That was Jack Weir in a nutshell: confident, nervy, quick witted, and very bright. He didn't succeed with Barlow, but he made his point, and he provided a glimpse of himself as the counsel who never backed away from a challenge. He had no hesitation in speaking his mind when he was certain of his ground. Once, on a matter before the Ontario Municipal Board, when the board gave an oral ruling against Weir's client, he snapped, "You don't get that decision from the statute. You get it from a phone call."

Called to the bar in 1938, he had barely begun his practice when he left for the war overseas with the Queen's Own Rifles, where he saw active service in Northwest Europe and finished with the rank of major. Back in Toronto, setting out as a litigator in his own small firm, he appeared in a trial pitted against George Gale of Mason, Foulds. "Weir was so good he almost frightened Gale," John Arnup later reported. "So we thought we'd better go after him to join our firm."

No one could miss Weir when he walked into the office, not on the first day and not on the thousands of days afterwards. Weir was the man with the infectious laugh that echoed down the corridors. He was small in stature but resonant in presence. He won affection as well as respect from his colleagues, and, among their wives, Weir was the favourite. He

radiated sociability and was genuinely curious about each person's life and interests. No one resisted Weir's charm.

His strength as a counsel lay in his powers of persuasion. He possessed a deep knowledge of the law, basing his approach on first principles. "He could give you a fundamental legal principle," a colleague at the firm said, "and he could trace its history from Richard the Lion-Heart all the way up to the day before yesterday." But it was the powerful manner in which he handled the principles, the strength of his presentation, that particularly separated him from other counsel. Weir was the great persuader.

He handled agency work for out-of-town solicitors and for Toronto firms that lacked litigation departments of their own. He kept busy in Weekly Court and in the Court of Appeal. But, gradually, he began to establish his name as the pre-eminent counsel in municipal law. He became expert in the workings of city councils. He attended to planning matters and appeared before the Ontario Municipal Board more often than any other counsel. He advised city solicitors, planning boards, and elected officials, learning to gauge the politics and propensities of every councilor and every bureaucrat. He knew the people and he knew the issues, and he understood how the two fit together.

Weir was a man of many roles. He adhered devoutly to the Catholic faith he was born into and served as president of the Catholic Children's Aid Society of Metro Toronto. He was a competitive sailor, though legend had it that four boats sank under him in four different races. He had a term as president of the Canadian Bar Association and demonstrated his zeal for the job by taking a Berlitz course in French in order to better represent the CBA's Quebec members.

Weir attacked every aspect of his life and his profession with the same unwavering resolve. He never for a moment doubted his ability to persuade. On a day when he needed an injunction on very short notice, he stepped into Madame Justice Mabel Van Camp's chambers and suggested she endorse the injunction on the back of an envelope that Weir offered from his pocket. He said he would file the proper material in support as soon as possible. As requested, Justice Van Camp signed the endorsement on the envelope. Weir expected nothing less. No one turned Weir down when he was in full flight – except Justice Fred Barlow on a mandamus application one morning in the mid-1950s.

John Mirsky (1914–1962)

Jack Mirsky and his brother Mervin were identical twins, even including the broken noses both received as teenage football players at Ottawa's Glebe Collegiate.

The identicalness came in handy for Jack, the cagey criminal lawyer, on the day in the 1950s when he double-booked himself, one case in Magistrates' Court in downtown Ottawa in the morning, another in a court up the Ottawa Valley in the afternoon. When the Ottawa judge put over the announcement of his decision to the afternoon, Jack summoned his businessman brother to substitute for him while he hurried up the valley. Jack's instructions to Mervin were to sit very still at the counsel's table and say as little as was politely possible. Mervin followed orders. The judge announced his ruling, which favoured Jack's client. Mervin nodded his thanks (actually he was nodding Jack's thanks), and nobody in the courtroom was any the wiser. Jack considered it a day's work well done.

It helped Jack's cause on the occasion of the great substitution that Mervin had a lawyer's training earlier in life. The twin brothers were the sons of an immigrant father of no education and monumental industry who founded a soft-drink company that grew into the hugely successful Pure Springs Canada Limited. The father, keen that his sons acquire the learning he was never permitted, sent the twins to the University of Toronto and to Osgoode Hall, both receiving their calls in 1939. Mervin practised briefly before serving as an officer in the Second World War; on his discharge, he joined Pure Springs and ran the company for decades. Jack, meanwhile, prevented from taking part in the war by a degenerative disk condition, set immediately on the adventure in

the law that made him the king of Ottawa's criminal courts and a figure of much respect at the city's bar.

Mirsky's long-time partner, Hy Soloway, was a brilliant commercial lawyer, and the firm built by the two men flourished in many fields. But Mirsky's heart belonged to his criminal practice and, to Soloway's frequent chagrin, the waiting room was filled with members of the beleaguered underclass. They were Mirsky's people, the clients of a counsel who preferred the police court to the boardroom. Mirsky was smart, scrappy but fair, a tough cross-examiner and a diligent student of the *Criminal Code*. He tended to his share of civil litigation and was an expert in municipal law, but it was criminal law he practised with a vengeance, a counsel who balanced dozens of active cases in his mind at any one time.

Mirsky's manner in the courtroom was based on a sense of ease, a man as confident, thoughtful, and engaging as if he were entertaining guests in his own home. When Judge Livius Sherwood was conducting his very first case in Provincial Court, he was visibly nervous and anxious. It happened that Mirsky was the defence counsel that day. Immediately aware of Sherwood's distress, Mirsky rose and asked the judge to take judicial notice that Ottawa Transportation buses never stopped at a stop sign. Sherwood recognized the intentional silliness of the remark and burst out in laughter. He relaxed, and for the rest of his long service on the bench he was grateful for Mirsky's act of kindness.

Mirsky was popular among his fellow counsel. He was a regular at Murray's Restaurant on Elgin Street, where lawyers gathered each day for lunch. He entertained with stories of his one hobby, riding his three-gaited horse, Laddie, at the stables over on Aylmer Road. In 1962 his fellow lawyers elected him president of the Carleton Law Association, a rare honour for a lawyer known principally for criminal work. At the time, Mirsky was approaching the height of his career, the head of a firm – Mirsky, Soloway, Assaly and Houston – that had gained recognition as one of the most versatile in Ottawa.

Then, in the early spring of that year, Mirsky was killed in an auto accident, his life cut short when he was just forty-seven years old. At his funeral procession, leaving from the synagogue on King Edward Avenue, a large contingent of Ottawa Police Service officers joined the procession of mourners. It was one of many signs of the affection and respect Mirsky had attracted from all sides in his brief but splendid time in the courts.

John Malcolm Robb (1917–1981)

The most lasting and intense influence on Malcolm Robb's career as a litigator came during his articling years. He articled with the legendary counsel Arthur Slaght, who became both mentor and older friend to Robb.

He invited Robb into his home and, over meals, Slaght passed on his tricks of the trade. When Robb went out on his own, Slaght sent him off with the transcripts of several Slaght trials. Robb saved the transcripts all his life, studying them, sometimes showing them to younger counsel, urging them to read the transcripts as lessons in the way a real lawyer conducted a trial. Robb was in awe of the man who had been his senior. He modelled himself on Slaght so completely that more than one lawyer pointed out to Robb that his signature looked exactly like Slaght's.

Robb's forte was in examination-in-chief. He liked to think of himself as a master cross-examiner, but he came to the realization that it was more essential to lay out his own case for the trier of fact in a trial, civil or criminal, in smooth and clear fashion. So it was that when Robb rose in court to present his side of a case, it was with no fumbling of papers and no asking of questions that confused his witnesses. Robb was prepared. His presentation was organized, timely, and in the correct sequence. Chronology meant everything to Robb. And

He was a devoted reader of the All-England Reports, searching out odd pieces of law that might be unknown to other counsel, anything that could provide Robb with an edge before the judge.

if his sense of order dazzled the courtroom to such a degree that Robb was able to slide in leading questions without raising an objection from the Crown or the judge, so much the better. It was one of the lessons he had learned from Arthur Slaght.

Though Robb's call to the bar came in 1939, his practice was delayed by the Second World War, in which he served with heroism. He joined the RCAF and flew Spitfires in combat. He was promoted to flight lieutenant and became the recipient of a Distinguished Flying Cross. By war's end, he was so anxious to get back in his lawyer's harness that he passed the time waiting for his discharge in England by volunteering to conduct court martials, an experience he relished.

Returning to Canada, he set up a practice with three younger counsel in Belleville, Ontario. Toronto was his ultimate destination, but, for seven years, he honed his skills in the smaller centre. He developed his precise style, animated by a broad streak of combativeness, and he was generous in sharing his ideas with the juniors in the Belleville office. Then, in 1954, he headed home to Toronto, where he practised on his own for the rest of his career, taking both civil and criminal cases.

Robb cut a fine figure in the courtroom, a counsel born to wear the gown. He was an impressive-looking man, and he kept his gown, vest, dickey, and tabs immaculate and freshly laundered. He was a demon for self-improvement, alert to upgrade his courtroom skills in ways that might strike other counsel as off-beat. He joined a weekly talk group where members had their turns delivering speeches. Robb's motivation was to streamline his form in addressing juries, and he took lessons in ballroom dancing to give himself a better sense of grace in the courtroom.

He was a devoted reader of the *All-England Reports*, searching out odd pieces of law that might be unknown to other counsel, anything that could provide Robb with an edge before the judge. He developed theories that, as far as he was concerned, covered everything he needed to know about occupational groups. His theories explained the nature of doctors, lawyers, and Indian chiefs, and, once a theory was in place, Robb was immovable on the subject.

He was aggressive, even belligerent, in court. On one memorable occasion, he arranged for a sheriff's officer to serve a notice of motion on Judge Ian Macdonnell, prohibiting Macdonnell from proceeding with a drug trial in which Robb's client was the accused. "For cold-blooded effrontery and discourtesy," Macdonnell thundered in court, "I have never seen anything to equal this in my twenty-five years on the bench!"

Robb took Macdonnell's words as a badge of honour. He might have thought that Arthur Slaght would have done the same thing.

Willard Zebedee Estey (1919–2002)

To almost everybody, he was "Bud" on first meeting, an open, engaging, bright man of enormous energy.

He could crack jokes about all subjects, but he was completely earnest when he said of the profession he practised, "If Canada didn't have the British inheritance of an independent bar, we would be just another banana republic." Estey knew what he was talking about from his own vast experience and from his family's outstanding history in the law.

His father, James, was a New Brunswicker who studied law at Harvard, then went west to Saskatchewan in 1915. He taught at the province's university, won election as a Liberal to the provincial legislature, served as attorney general, and capped his career with an appointment to the Supreme Court of Canada, where he sat with distinction from 1944 to 1956.

The younger Estey had no intention of following in his learned father's footsteps. He planned on taking an MBA at Harvard and making his impact in business. But Harvard's fees were too steep, and Estey turned to law. He earned an LL.B. in Saskatchewan before he went off to the Second World War. He joined the army first, switched to the RCAF, and drew an assignment as one of the few Canadians to fly missions with the Americans over Japan.

In 1947, after a year of teaching at the University of Saskatchewan, he headed east. Thinking Toronto would become Canada's dominant centre of commerce, he hoped the city would provide the challenge of the most interesting legal issues. He was right on both counts. He joined the firm of Robertson, Fleury and Lane and reigned for the next twenty-

five years as the battling terror of corporate litigation. Tax and copyright cases were particularly to his taste. "The law in those fields was pure and clean," Estey said, "and when you got into inter-corporate battles, it was always related to a stake worth fighting for."

With CTV as a client, he fought a long and intricate case that set the record straight on the law applying to television performances of copyrighted music. In an equally lengthy and tangled case for Famous Players, he established precedents in the field of cable television. It was also at Famous Players that he got the chance to realize his early ambition to preside as a corporate boss.

"The way it ended up," he explained, "I was running the company nights and holidays and weekends, flying all over the world to keep the thing in business."

He switched professional gears in 1973 when he accepted an appointment to the Court of Appeal for Ontario. Estey later characterized that court, with its personnel in the 1970s, as "the best single court in the Western world." His own acumen and industry contributed to the court's lofty reputation, but he wasn't a man to stay in the same place for long. He moved to the Ontario High Court in 1975 as chief justice, and, a year later, he became chief justice of Ontario.

Estey was a happy man. "A courtroom is where the fun is," he said, "whether you're a counsel or a judge." He was a reformer as chief justice, a pusher and a prodder, clearing the backlog of reserved judgments and speeding up the process of justice. But he wasn't allowed to stay in the post for even a year. In September 1977 he was sworn in as a justice of the Supreme Court of Canada. For a son who didn't intend to duplicate his father's career, Estey managed the remarkable feat of ending up in the same courtroom where James Estey had completed his own life in the law.

Bud Estey brought enthusiasm to the court. He supplied a sensible voice to the immense constitutional questions that the Supreme Court considered and answered in the early 1980s. And he remained active in his life away from the court – a skier, a tennis player, the man who dashed around the country as president of Hockey Canada.

"Life is so full of activity," he said, in the words that summed up his career, "that I never have time to get tired of any of it."

McLeod Archibald Craig (1917–2003)

Around Owen Sound, the locals used to say that Mac Craig was the first person in town to read each day's *Globe and Mail*.

By the time he got to the office in the morning, he was up to the minute on politics, sports, and world events and raring to hash over the news with anyone he encountered. Craig took the same keen attitude to the law. He read the latest case reports, the most recent learned articles, and the newest textbooks dealing with the fields that engaged him. He couldn't get enough of legal issues, and he was the most eager member in every group of lawyers who gathered to talk shop. As one of his Owen Sound partners said, Craig was a man in love with the law.

The love affair began early in Craig's life. He grew up in the small town of Paisley, northwest of Walkerton, and when he left home for the University of Toronto (where he starred in hockey for the Varsity Blues), he chose the Honours Law course. At Osgoode Hall he was a member of the class of 1942, but he wasn't around on the day of his call to the bar. By then he had left for Europe with the West Nova Scotia Regiment to fight in the Second World War.

It was in the army, during the campaign in northern Italy in 1944, that Craig got his first taste of the courtroom. A soldier in his regiment was charged with rape, and Craig acted for the defence at the soldier's court martial. The prosecutor summoned a roster of witnesses, but he neglected one element: he failed to ask a single witness to identify Craig's client as the accused man in the case. Craig seized on the technicality and won a dismissal of the charge.

Two years later, after Craig recovered from wounds he suffered in Italy and his discharge from service with the rank of captain, he took up practice in the Walkerton firm headed by Campbell Grant. Grant was the pre-eminent litigator in Bruce County, and, though Craig handled the usual assortment of a small-town lawyer's duties, he wanted a practice

He brought the same competitive edge to argument as he had to hockey in his Varsity years. He was prepared and he was methodical, but, most of all, he was forcefully persistent. He thrilled to the adversarial process, and he was the counsel who loved the law.

similar to Grant's. His big break came in 1952, when Owen Sound's number one litigator, Fred MacKay, received an appointment to the Court of Appeal. Craig was invited to fill the vacuum left by MacKay, and, for the next two-and-a-half decades, he thrived as Owen Sound's leading man of the courts.

He took murder cases and every variety of civil litigation. He acted for plaintiffs and defendants in personal injury claims. In all ways possible, he indulged his grand romance with the law. He entered enthusiastically into issues that touched on rural life: he served as counsel on a provincial inquiry into the bankruptcy of a farmers' co-op and another inquiry into the distribution of fruit and vegetables in the province. He sat for two years on the Ontario Milk Commission. As far as Craig was concerned, all activities that took him before a decision-making body, whether it was in a courtroom or in a hearing room, were welcome.

His style in argument was built on persistence. No judge and no commission chairman could shake Craig. To him, if a point was worth making once, it was worth making two or three more times. He brought the same competitive edge to argument as he had to hockey in his Varsity years. He was prepared and he was methodical, but, most of all, he was forcefully persistent. He thrilled to the adversarial process, and he was the counsel who loved the law.

It was always part of his life's plan to move to the bench, and that ambition was realized when the Trudeau government appointed him to the Trial Division of the Supreme Court in 1976. Craig took as much deep-rooted satisfaction in sitting in judgment on arguments as he formerly had in presenting them. He remained on the bench until his mandatory retirement in 1992. Then he took his unquenchable sense of competition, and splendid athletic skills, to the golf course. He also continued to be the quickest man in any company to finish reading the *Globe and Mail*.

Allan Goodman (1921–1997)

The Liberal government of Pierre Trudeau appointed Allan Goodman to the Trial Division of the Ontario Supreme Court in 1973. Six years later, Joe Clark's Tory government promoted Goodman to the Court of Appeal.

What made both appointments remarkable was that Goodman happened to be a committed member of the NDP.

Goodman spent his lifetime confounding expectations and overcoming obstacles. His father, a Polish immigrant, died when Allan was two years old, and his mother when he was sixteen. With the support of his five older siblings, he worked his way through McMaster University in his Hamilton hometown and through Osgoode Hall, where he won the gold medal in his year of graduation, 1943. On convocation day, one of Goodman's sisters collected his medal, because the RCAF had taken her brother into service for the Second World War.

In 1946 Goodman made what might seem an odd choice for a gold medalist: he set up a one-man practice in the town of Welland, Ontario. But Goodman thrived as the consummate small-town lawyer. He drew wills, appeared in police court, and handled labour matters, including the negotiation of contracts for police associations in southern Ontario. He topped the polls when he ran for Welland's town council, serving seven years as an alderman, and later he chaired the local water commission. Though he was modest and unassuming, people around town recognized that Goodman was the wise man in their midst, the fellow who had the sharpest insights when he gathered with his cronies in law and business over morning cups of coffee at the Reeta Hotel.

By the 1960s, while Goodman remained a generalist, he had developed a particular reputation for his skill in the criminal courts. His courtroom manner mirrored the man: he spoke in a soft voice, he radiated a quiet authority, and his grasp of the law was thorough and apt. Goodman's preparation could never be faulted, and, among his criminal cases that originated in the Welland courts, more than a few resonated far beyond the town.

Goodman's sensitivity was particularly apparent in his defence of a local doctor charged with the attempted murder

of his wife. The wife suffered terribly from terminal cancer, and the doctor, unable to bear his wife's agony, tried to end her pain and her life by surreptitiously feeding her rat poison. When the plan failed and the doctor was charged, Goodman presented the court with a reasoned defence of attempted euthanasia. "My client is more to be pitied than punished" became the mantra of Goodman's argument. It failed to gain an acquittal, but it won a short sentence, just six months, a term brief enough to allow the doctor to return to his wife in her last days.

Then there was the case of the two Welland taxi drivers who offered a service placing bets for customers at the nearby Fort Erie Racetrack. The customers gave the cabbies written instructions, including the name of the horse, the sum, and the type of bet. In return for a percentage of the winnings, the cabbies handled the rest. The police charged the pair with engaging in the business of betting contrary to the *Criminal Code*. First in Magistrates' Court, then in the Court of Appeal, Goodman presented the argument that, in order to commit the offence, his clients would have to make the bets on their own premises. He argued that the cab drivers placed the bets at the racetrack just as though their customers were betting in person. The Appeal Court accepted the argument and, with the victory, Goodman helped pave the way to the legalization of off-track betting in Ontario.

In his later years as a judge, Goodman never used a clerk. He didn't need anyone to look up the law because no case came before him where he hadn't already dealt with the issues during his career as a generalist. When his daughter Susie joined the profession and then went to the bench, she could phone her father at any hour of the day or night with every conceivable legal problem. Goodman always picked up on the second ring and always had the answers. They were all in the head of the modest man of the law.

Charles Leonard Dubin (b. 1921)

When clients applied to Charles Dubin, he drew no lines. He defended a Thunder Bay dog named Rex who faced death under the *Vicious Animals Act*; the dog got off.

He represented Prime Minister John Diefenbaker at the inquiry into the Gerda Munsinger affair; nobody laid a glove on Dief. He represented a Toronto Argonaut star halfback named Dave Mann at a trial on a charge of possession of marijuana; Mann was acquitted. "I acted for bookies and for major corporations," Dubin once said in describing the range of his clients. Nor was his practice confined to criminal law. Perhaps more than any other leading counsel of his generation, he maintained an astonishing balance of both criminal and civil cases, moving in a seemingly effortless fashion between the two disciplines.

At the beginning of his career, he represented unions in labour negotiations and litigation, but, in fairly short order, he took on corporate clients and, from then on, Dubin's firm was one of the few shops that worked for both management and labour. He was counsel to the *Toronto Telegram*, and he represented the Toronto Firefighters and Ontario Hydro's employees. He defended in fifteen capital murder trials, and he served as counsel to myriad government commissions and boards of inquiry. The ease of his versatility was remarkable, making it plain that he deserved the designation one judge had applied to him, "a complete man of the law." It was Dubin.

From the beginning, he was a bright young fellow on a very fast track. Born in Hamilton, he whizzed through the city's Central Collegiate Institute and earned a Bachelor of Arts at the University of Toronto when he was barely out of his teens. His call to the bar came in 1944, when, to the surprise of no one, he won the gold medal in his year. On graduation, he formed a firm with a classmate, J.R. Kimber, who handled the solicitor's work in the two-man operation while Dubin set out to make his mark in the courtroom. Six years later, at age twenty-nine, he became the youngest Queen's Counsel in the British Commonwealth.

Of all his talents as a counsel, his gift for cross-examination stood out. Dubin, a man who dominated the courtroom without making the slightest fuss about it, seemed to have antennae of a magical sort in detecting falsehoods or bias in witnesses' testimony. He never failed to capitalize on such revelations, and he was equally adept in ferreting out the fallacies in testimony from those who believed they were recounting the truth. As in all aspects of a counsel's work, Dubin provided textbook examples of the cross-examinor's art.

In 1973 he was appointed to the Court of Appeal, becoming associate chief justice in 1987 and chief justice three years later, serving until 1996. During his distinguished period on the bench, he took time away from the court to preside over several commissions and inquiries. He handled the arbitration in the dispute between the Metro Toronto School Board and its teachers in 1976, and he chaired an investigation into procedures at the Hospital for Sick Children in 1983. Dubin appeared to draw the toughest of inquiries, no doubt because he possessed both common sense and a reassuring manner that inspired calm in those who appeared before him. That was notably the case in the inquiry of the late 1980s into the use of drugs in sport, which grew out of the Ben Johnson scandal at the Seoul Olympic Games. The extensive hearings lasted eleven months, much of them broadcast across the country on television, placing Dubin front and centre to millions of viewers. It represented a rare instance when Canada's most visible man of the law happened also to be one of its most accomplished.

Walter Bernard Williston (1919–1980)

Walter Williston charged at life as if he hadn't enough time to get everything done. To him, sleep represented wasted hours.

Much waited to be accomplished, and, in Williston's rush to encompass all that was available, he propelled himself to the front rank as a counsel, writer, teacher, mentor, and governor. And in carousing – in games played, fine meals consumed, expensive whiskeys downed – he was world class.

Born in China of Anglican missionary parents, Williston spent his teenage years in northern Ontario. He took the Honours Law course at the University of Toronto, then attended Osgoode Hall, receiving his call to the bar in 1944. He joined the Fasken firm, where he had articled, and remained a Fasken man for his entire career, minus one year, 1948–49, which he spent as a full-time lecturer at Osgoode. In all the remaining years he assumed a prodigious load of litigation, and, in the process, he attracted to Faskens a roster of gifted young counsel not surpassed by any other Toronto firm.

In just his third year at the bar, Williston took an appeal to the Privy Council. It was a case that Williston's client had lost at trial and on appeal, and at the Privy Council he was opposed by the formidable Arthur Slaght. With the odds seemingly against him, the youthful Williston was so decisive in victory that the law lords asked him, as a hypothetical matter, how he would have presented Slaght's side of the argument. Williston obliged, their lordships were grateful, and Williston's client was ecstatic.

Williston operated with a courtroom manner that was deceptive and unconventional. He often stammered, but the

apparently garbled delivery worked uncannily in his favour. Judges ended up completing Williston's sentences for him, finishing with the very point that he wanted them to adopt. One of Williston's many splendid juniors, John Sopinka, accurately described his senior's style in the courts as "a kind of homespun sincerity."

Williston's dedication to his profession went far beyond his courtroom mastery. He published invaluable textbooks dealing with matters of civil procedure. He continued to lecture part time at Osgoode, at one point teaching, of all unlikely subjects, family law. In his long service as a bencher, he assumed the lead in introducing specialization into the profession, together with the right to advertise the specialty.

On two remarkable occasions, he stepped away from his own principal field of civil litigation to take the appeals in capital murder cases. In the first, in 1950, he used the issue of provocation to win a new trial for a Napanee man sentenced to death for murdering his wife; at the retrial, the man was found guilty of manslaughter. The second appeal, in 1962, was on behalf of Arthur Lucas, the Detroit man condemned to be hanged for a Toronto murder. Williston, convinced of Lucas' innocence, threw all his powers and passion into the case, but both the Court of Appeal and the Supreme Court of Canada refused the appeal. The distraught Williston was the last outside visitor to offer comfort to Lucas before he was executed at the Don Jail.

Williston had an extraordinary capacity for concentration. He loved to talk tactics with his juniors, analyze evidence, weigh alternatives, micromanage everything from the order of witnesses in a trial to the sequence of arguments in an appeal. His eye for talent was unerring, as was the eye of his partner, Ron Rolls, and the list of counsel who put in years as both men's juniors included people whose later careers took them to the Supreme Court of Canada (Sopinka) and to the federal cabinet (Allan Rock, Bill Graham).

To be Williston's junior involved demands beyond the norm. Williston led all hands in early morning tennis and late nights over dinner and drinks. He insisted on trips to Pogue's Gym on Bay Street, where Williston startled everyone by routinely bench-pressing 250 pounds. When he had an appeal before the Supreme Court in Ottawa, he was known to drive from Toronto in a convertible, the top down no matter what the weather. Walter Williston was the counsel who never went less than full tilt at life and the law.

Walter Williston was president of The Advocates' Society from 1969 to 1971.

Arthur Edward Martin Maloney (1919–1984)

Arthur Maloney was alone in a City Hall elevator on September 17, 1952, when Chief Justice James McRuer happened to step on board.

In five days, McRuer would begin to hear the trial of Steve Suchan and Leonard Jackson, the two notorious Toronto bank robbers who were charged with the murder of a police detective. John Robinette represented Suchan. Jackson had no counsel. On the elevator, from out of the blue, McRuer asked Maloney to take Jackson's case. The young lawyer, hardly in a position to turn down the chief justice, accepted the assignment. It was a trial that changed Maloney's life.

At the time, he was a little known but promising counsel who had never argued a capital case. By the end of the widely publicized Suchan-Jackson trial, with the conviction of the two accused and their hanging at the Don Jail, Maloney emerged as a high-profile defence lawyer and a sadder, wiser man. A devout Catholic, he acquired an even deeper appreciation for the value of human life, and he came away from the case with such an abiding opposition to capital punishment that he made himself the tireless and successful champion of its abolition in Canada.

Born into a large Ottawa Valley family of Irish Canadians, Maloney was sentimental and loquacious, a gregarious drinker in his prime, a man with the common touch in and out of court. His favourite 1950s bar was in downtown Toronto's Metropole Hotel, a rowdy spot that attracted truck drivers, rounders, newspapermen, cops, and Maloney's lawyer crowd. He connected with each of the Metropole's drinking constituencies, just as, in the courtroom, he spoke a layman's language that persuaded juries of ordinary citizens to identify with him and his causes.

Maloney always said he was no great shakes as a student at Osgoode Hall Law School, and later he downplayed his own knowledge of the law. But from early in his career, he grasped the strategies and concepts necessary to be an accomplished criminal lawyer. He displayed unusual patience in his cross-examinations, conveying the impression he had all day in waiting out a witness. And he developed an uncanny talent for effecting a seamless flow from the witnesses' testimony to his sensible jury addresses. The addresses seemed in his hands to be less an argument and more a mutual search, Maloney and the jurors together, after the truth.

In one remarkable 1954 murder trial in Port Arthur, the Crown appeared to have an unbeatable case against Maloney's client. But Maloney destroyed the prosecution entirely on his cross-examinations of the Crown witnesses. He called no witnesses in defence, and the jury needed just thirty minutes to acquit. At another out-of-the-ordinary capital trial in Toronto in 1963, Maloney argued a defence of automatism in what appeared on the surface to be a certain Crown victory. Again the jurors, eagerly embracing Maloney's interpretation of events as the reasonable explanation, required little time in returning a verdict of not guilty.

Despite his pre-eminence at the criminal bar – plus the occasional fruitful foray into civil work – Maloney occasionally grew restless in the law. He wanted more involvement in the life of his country, and he reached for other roles. From 1957 to 1962 he sat as the Progressive Conservative MP for the Toronto riding of Parkdale. More than a decade later, in 1975, the Ontario Tory government named Maloney the province's first ombudsman, a job to which he brought a lifetime of sticking up for the underdog.

Alas for Maloney, and for the public that regarded him as one of its own, both jobs ended in disappointment through no fault of Maloney's. In Ottawa, Prime Minster John Diefenbaker failed to name him to the cabinet, an appointment Maloney had many reasons to expect. And his time in the ombudsman's post was cut short, in large part as a result of political and bureaucratic stalemates.

In Maloney's later years, even in illness, his curiosity remained active and searching. He was fascinated by myriad subjects, from the miracle of Fatima to the workings of his 350-acre farm northwest of Toronto. But it was to criminal law that he responded most vividly, and, when he died in 1984, he left behind a reputation as a counsel of uncommon resourcefulness, intelligence, and commitment to his clients.

Arthur Maloney was president of The Advocates' Society in 1973–74.

Sydney Lewis Robins (b. 1923)

Syd Robins listened to his parents' advice. His mother and his father, a Toronto businessman born in Russia, emphasized education, telling their son that schooling led to achievement in life. Young Syd agreed.

He took the Honours Law course at the University of Toronto. That gave him a Bachelor of Arts. In first year at Osgoode Hall Law School, he simultaneously attended extra courses at Varsity, which led to a Bachelor of Laws. When he finished Osgoode and received his call to the bar in 1947, he went off to Harvard, where he earned a Master's in law.

Back in Toronto, recognition that Robins was a scholar came quickly and unexpectedly. Cecil Wright, the eminent Osgoode teacher, fell ill and, to replace him as the lecturer in torts, the law school turned to Robins, who, at twenty-four, was barely older than his new students. He was a success and continued for a dozen years as a part-time teacher at Osgoode, taking the torts classes and heading the practice groups, which were the precursor of the Bar Admission course. The qualities that made him an effective lecturer – elegance, grace, lucidity – were the same qualities that came to define him as a counsel. Robins took immense care with his preparation in the courtroom, as in the classroom: his appearance and speech inspired confidence in students and clients alike, and his talent for cutting to the core of an issue ensured that his content always measured up to his presentation.

Robins had articled with the Chitty, McMurtry firm under Roy McMurtry Sr., who had a highly active practice in personal injury work. This experience gave Robins his first large taste for the courtroom and confirmed him in his decision to make litigation the basis of his own practice. He began as a one-man operation, gradually expanding into a busy firm that included his younger brother Hartley. If the Robins group was noted for one particular field, it was its labour practice, and, for that, Robins owed his old teacher and associate Cecil Wright.

Wright, as impressed by Robins' advocacy as by his teaching, referred a Teamsters' matter to the Robins office. When the Teamsters expressed themselves delighted with the way Robins handled the file, word got around the labour community that the bright young counsel was someone to rely on. In due course, Robins became general counsel to the Toronto Building Council and found his days occupied with hearings before the Labour Relations Board and with a broad spectrum of negotiations and trials in which he represented labour's cause.

Yet, demonstrating his even-handedness as an advocate, Robins maintained equally congenial relations with the business community, and his practice came to reflect an astounding diversity. He acted for land developers, and he took a significant case all the way to the Supreme Court of Canada for the financier Max Tanenbaum. For the Crown, he prosecuted a dozen paving companies on price-fixing charges, and, early in his career, he represented a client named Maker in a matter that unexpectedly contributed to the expansion of Ed Mirvish's merchandising empire. Mr. Maker, who lived in a semi-detached on Markham Street south of Honest Ed's store on Bloor Street, had a weak heart and needed his afternoon naps. But the other half of his house was occupied by the noisy washing-machine division of Honest Ed's. Robins sued Mirvish on behalf of Maker, claiming an unreasonable use of land in a residential area. When Robins obtained an injunction against Mirvish, Honest Ed was in trouble because Christmas was just around the corner. How was he supposed to sell his Christmas washing machines? Mirvish's answer was to move immediately and buy Maker's semi-detached. The purchase eventually led him to snap up the rest of the Markham block and create his profitable Mirvish Village of cafés, bookstores, and artists' studios. Robins thought the intriguing little case had a happy ending for all parties.

Robins' gifts as an advocate paved the way to achievements in other roles. He became the first Jewish treasurer of the Law Society, and, in 1976, he went to the Supreme Court of Ontario, first in the Trial Division, then in the Court of Appeal. His career added up to successes that would have pleased but not surprised his parents, who had sent their son into the world with the wisest advice he ever received.

David Gondran Humphrey (b. 1925)

Dave Humphrey's client faced a rape charge. As the trial unfolded, it became clear that the evidence against the client lacked substance.

The Crown's case, weak to begin with, developed holes. Humphrey pondered his address to the jury and, in the end, he confined himself to a one-sentence statement: "Members of the jury," he said, "if this case is rape, then I'm a monkey's uncle, and though the resemblance may be amazing, I ain't."

Humphrey was the rare criminal lawyer who knew how to use humour as a forensic tool, and, with him, there was always a method to the mirth. In the rape trial, he reasoned that a lengthy and impassioned address might cause the jury to wonder if there was more to the case than they thought. Humphrey went with the funny one-liner. The jury took no time in acquitting.

The laughs constituted only one weapon in Humphrey's regular arsenal. He was intuitively brilliant in sizing up the psychological terrain of a courtroom, calculating how judge and jury reacted viscerally to his client, and trimming his case to fit the attitudes. With his breezy manner, he made easy connections with the Crown witnesses. The breeziness put the witnesses at ease during cross-examination; it also set them up for a surprise when Humphrey changed his manner and went for the jugular.

Sometimes Humphrey, an avid motorcyclist, read Harley-Davidson magazines in court. To him, that was no big deal. He was waiting out the presentation of evidence that he considered useless to his case. He was a fervent believer in discarding lesser defences and settling on just one possible winning point of argument. In court, he let the irrelevant evidence pass by, turning the pages of his magazine and giving the impression he hadn't a care in the world, until the time came for him to pounce with his single powerful defence.

As a young man, he drove a cab in Toronto and joined the United States Navy to see the world. Both experiences gave him insights into the seamier sides of life and, when he received his call to the bar in 1949, he headed straight for criminal

practice. He defended in countless murder cases; he represented both mobsters and cops in trouble; he took humble legal aid clients and such mighty corporate giants as Amway. He worked on intuition in the courtroom, and he depended on intellectual inspiration. In the early 1960s he defended a woman charged with perjury as a result of her refusal to identify in court the men she saw at close range while they committed a vicious assault on another man; Humphrey conceived of a defence, unique to the time, of hysterical amnesia. The imaginative argument won the woman's acquittal.

Humphrey possessed a rascal's streak. It was he, the opera buff, who, alone among members of a Massey Hall audience at a Maria Callas concert, dropped a boo among the bravas. And it was Humphrey, standing on the sidelines of the 1957 Grey Cup game at Varsity Stadium, who stuck out his foot and tripped a Hamilton Tiger Cat defensive back named Bibbles Bawel while he was running down the field with an intercepted pass. Years later, when Bibbles Bawel and his interception were long forgotten, when even the score of the game had faded from memory, the story of the legendary trip resonated among members of the criminal bar who were always alert to an entertaining Humphrey adventure.

A man of many sides, Humphrey knew his Bible and taught Sunday School for years at a Presbyterian church. His love of golf matched his enthusiasm for opera. He sailed an Albacore as deftly as he steered his motorcycle. He generated affection among his peers and had a quick eye for spotting young talent, taking on students and juniors who proceeded to bright careers as defence counsel. His own colourful career included his appointment in 1985 to the bench, a role he had earned beyond question but one he may not have anticipated when he began his life in the law among criminal lawyers.

Bert James MacKinnon (1921–1987)

Bert MacKinnon liked to describe himself as just a poor beekeeper's son from St. Eugene, Ontario.

The description had the merit of truth – his father was an apiarist in a small town near Ottawa – but the reason MacKinnon worked the line so often was because he identified with people who came out of nowhere and made a contribution to the life around them. MacKinnon was one of those people, the Baptist son of a small farmer who contributed remarkably to the bar, the bench, and the country. He lived what he believed, a moralist but not a hypocrite.

His duty to Canada came early, when, fresh out of McMaster University, he served four wartime years in the Canadian Navy. Afterwards, he went to Oxford University on a Rhodes Scholarship, then to Osgoode Hall. Called to the bar in 1949, he joined the Toronto firm of Wright & McTaggart and began to forge a reputation as a masterful and distinctive litigator.

To MacKinnon, nirvana was taking three good points of law and arguing them before the Court of Appeal. Or, even better, arguing them before the Supreme Court of Canada; he liked nine people barking at him more than three. He handled trial work and served as counsel on many inquiries (notably the investigation into the Pickering Airport, at which he represented the federal government); but he could grow impatient with the trial process, and it was the appeal courts where he placed himself in his true arena. He was quick and intense in argument, one of the fastest of counsel at grasping the essence of a point. And he could be foxy, a quality that was often necessary in dealing with the tough characters on the Ontario appellate court in the years when MacKinnon flourished. He knew, for example, that Justice Walter Schroeder loved Latin; thus, MacKinnon deliberately worked Latin maxims into his arguments whether the maxims were relevant or not. Naturally, Schroeder came to adore MacKinnon.

Around his firm, MacKinnon was a hands-on instructor. He made it a habit to read and research his law in the firm library, sitting in a chair with his legs tucked under him, talking about cases with the students and sharing his encyclopedic legal knowledge.

MacKinnon read his own law and wrote his own factums. Before he went to court, he argued the case dozens of time to his juniors and to himself. By the time he reached the courtroom, he had worked himself into a fervour of total conviction in his case. With MacKinnon, the argument wasn't dispassionate; it came from a moral belief in the justness of his cause.

Around his firm, MacKinnon was a hands-on instructor. He made it a habit to read and research his law in the firm library, sitting in a chair with his legs tucked under him, talking about cases with the students and sharing his encyclopedic legal knowledge. He took phone calls from clients in the library, allowing the students to hear how he reacted to situations as they unfolded. To MacKinnon, a natural-born teacher, the phone calls were part of the process. He had an acute eye for talent, and an astonishing number of MacKinnon students and juniors, in whom he took enormous pride, went on to careers that saw them appointed to the Court of Appeal, the Federal Court, and the Supreme Court of Canada.

MacKinnon joined the Court of Appeal in 1975, and was named associate chief justice three years later. In the job, he became an important recruit among the new judges who were recreating the court from the abrupt and impatient old days of Schroeder and company. As a judge, MacKinnon carried on in the same style he had demonstrated as a counsel: he was quick with questions in the courtroom, prompt and thorough in writing reasons, and generous in mentoring younger colleagues.

MacKinnon's one great escape for relaxation from work as a lawyer and a judge came on his farm near Brighton, Ontario. His five children gathered at the place, which MacKinnon fixed up with a tennis court and a swimming pool. But he occupied himself in one other less conventional activity on the farm, an activity that was entirely appropriate to the MacKinnon life story: he kept bees.

Charles Terrence Murphy (b. 1926)

When Terry Murphy stood up in the Court of Appeal on March 11, 1953, he made a small piece of Ontario legal history.

Two months earlier, back home in Sault Ste. Marie, a Murphy client and another man were convicted of murdering a retired railroad engineer and sentenced to be hanged. Murphy appealed, and the instant he got to his feet in the Court of Appeal, he became the first lawyer from the Sault ever to argue such an appeal in person. Until then, all Sault lawyers had retained Toronto counsel. But history wasn't what Murphy had on his mind that day; he was more intent on winning the appeal. The principal evidence against the two convicted men consisted of statements, given by each to the police, claiming that the other man did the killing. Murphy conceded to the court that the evidence might warrant a conclusion that one or the other of the men had committed the crime. But no evidence existed that enabled the court to determine which one was responsible, and, therefore, the appeal court was obliged to quash the convictions and direct acquittals of the two appellants. The five-member court agreed with the argument, and it was this decision that played a major role in launching the career of twenty-five-year-old Terry Murphy as Sault Ste. Marie's pre-eminent criminal counsel for the next quarter century.

It became a legend among other lawyers around the courts that Terry Murphy could run a defence from the notes he made on the lined flap in a package of Players cigarettes. That's all he needed, the lawyers said; the rest was in his head.

An Irish Catholic, the son of the manager of a Sault men's clothing store, Murphy studied for a year at St. Peter's Seminary in London, Ontario, before he realized the priesthood wasn't his calling. He switched to an Arts course at Assumption College in Windsor, then Osgoode Hall, and, after his call to the bar in 1949, he headed back to the Sault to practise a little of every sort of law – particularly the sort that took him into the courtroom, where he felt most energized.

From the start, he was a counsel of confidence and legal smarts. It became a legend among other lawyers around the courts that Terry Murphy could run a defence from the notes he made on the lined flap in a package of Players cigarettes. That's all he needed, the lawyers said; the rest was in his head. Murphy conceded that he listened more than he wrote, that the only notes he made consisted of a phrase or two for use in his cross-examinations. But the real secret of his success lay in his knowledge of the rules of evidence; he knew them like the back of his hand. As for the legendary tale about the notes on the package of Players, Murphy pointed out that, personally, he smoked Winchesters.

He entered into a second piece of grim Sault history in 1955, when he defended one of two co-accused in another murder case. One of the two had killed a bank manager in the course of robbing the bank. He was charged with capital murder, and so was his partner in the stickup, who happened to be the shooter's sixteen-year-old son. Murphy represented the teenager, but both accused were convicted and sentenced to the gallows. Murphy managed to obtain a commutation of the death sentence for the boy, but the father was hanged in the Sault's jail, the last man in the town ever to be executed.

In 1968 Murphy won election as a Liberal member of parliament in the first Trudeau government. He served on the Justice Committee and took a term as chair of the North Atlantic Assembly, a post that required him to visit all the NATO countries. On his trip to Rome, he realized one of his life's most satisfying moments: a private audience for himself and his wife with Pope Paul VI.

When he lost his parliamentary seat to the NDP candidate in the 1972 election, he returned to his Sault practice, once more the lawyer in town who conducted his cases from a couple of brief notes and a comprehensive grasp on the rules of evidence. In 1980 he went to the bench as the Superior Court justice responsible for Manitoulin Island, an appointment that meant a move from the Sault to new quarters in Sudbury. His amazingly absorbent memory for the facts of a case and its law made him as effective as a judge as it had as a counsel, back when he was a young lawyer with a propensity for making a little legal history.

John Patrick Nelligan (b. 1921)

John Nelligan wore his Sixth Canadian Infantry uniform to the garden party. It was the spring of 1942, and young Nelligan knew he would soon be heading overseas.

But for now, at the party in the University College quadrangle, he was celebrating with the other new Arts graduates from the University of Toronto. Over the punch and canapés, one of Nelligan's professors, Bora Laskin, who taught at the university at the time, asked him about plans for his career after the war. Nelligan answered that he was thinking of law. "Yes," Laskin said, "I think you'd make a good lawyer."

It was a small remark, almost casual, but in the next years, as Nelligan fought from Normandy through Belgium and Holland, he thought often of Laskin's words. They helped to carry him past the horrors of the Second World War, giving him a dream of a future beyond the fighting, and, when he returned to peacetime Toronto in 1946, he enrolled at Osgoode Hall.

Nelligan, a self-starter if there ever was one, hardly filled the role of the typical Osgoode student. He also found the time to write articles for the *Canadian Bar Review*, to assist a senior lawyer in carrying out a survey of the legal profession, and to teach an introductory law course to Commerce and Finance students at the university. On his call in 1949, Nelligan immediately packed in valuable courtroom experience, working as a junior with both Arthur Maloney and Edson Haines. He moved to Ottawa to join the Duncan McIlraith firm, then to begin his own one-man practice, which eventually grew into the eminent firm of Nelligan, O'Brien, Payne. Nelligan himself turned out to be as distinctive as a lawyer as he had been as a law student, becoming a counsel of remarkable conscience and ingenuity.

His career took in a startling panoply of cases. When a group of businessmen in the community of Eastview, near Ottawa, asked him to investigate the city's management in the early 1960s, it was Nelligan who uncovered a corrupt system in which the mayor kept his own special fund of parking-meter revenues and the city treasurer bought herself a car out of city money. Publicity from Nelligan's Eastview revelations caught the eye of a radical group from the Mine, Mill and Smelter Workers' Union who were seeking certification. They needed a brave counsel, and Nelligan proved to be their kind of man. He took up the Mine, Mill cause, and that task led to work for the Teamsters.

The principal of a public school retained Nelligan to defend him at a trial arising out of a pupil's allegations that the man had rubbed the boy's leg inappropriately. Nelligan staged a demonstration in the courtroom, showing that, given the size of the desks and chairs in the classroom, it was physically impossible for the principal to have touched the boy. The principal's job and reputation were saved, but that was just one of several cases in which Nelligan performed similar rescue missions. He represented Senator Hazen Argue, when Argue was summoned to answer alleged offences by the Senate Accounts Committee, and he defended the cabinet minister John Munro against charges of suspicious campaign donations from Indian bands. Cases in which Nelligan's clients were underdogs seemed to rouse the best in his advocacy.

In later years, Nelligan argued frequently before Bora Laskin in the Supreme Court of Canada. The Canadian Aero case represented one such argument, a case that dealt with the principles guiding the circumstances under which an employee might take intelligence from one employer to another. Nelligan, representing the employee in the case, won at trial and in the Court of Appeal. But in the Supreme Court of Canada, Laskin held against him – and Nelligan was convinced that Laskin had erred in his judgment. But whatever the result, it was clear that Laskin had understated in 1942 when he picked an adjective to describe Nelligan's possibilities as a lawyer. Nelligan became far more than "good." Throughout his career, he was nothing less than superb.

John Nelligan was president of The Advocates' Society in 1983-84.

Part Three

1950-1964

Fernand Laurent Gratton (1926–1997)

When Fern Gratton set off on the annual moose hunt in the country north of his Sudbury hometown, he carried a rare gun called a .300 Savage Magnum.

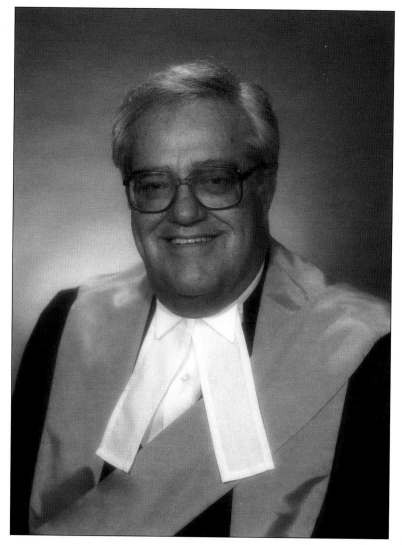

It was a powerful weapon, strong enough, his friends said, to stop an elephant. Fern never came home without his moose. The gun represented the flip side of Gratton, the opposite of his style in the courtroom. As a litigator, he was polished, subtle, and thorough. Around Sudbury, his colleagues at the bar called him the local guy with the silver tongue. He was a plaintiffs' lawyer, the king of the French Canadian practice in town, and he seldom – many said never – lost a jury case on his home turf.

Gratton was born in the nearby town of Chelmsford, the son of the postmaster. He studied at Sudbury's Sacred Heart College and at Laval University in Quebec City before heading off to Osgoode Hall. He articled with Leo Landreville in Sudbury, received his call to the bar in 1950, set himself up in practice, and never took a backward step.

Good manners became Gratton's forte in the courtroom. He developed a polite and polished style in presenting his case, never permitting the sweat he had poured into his preparation to show itself. In Gratton's early days, a couple of the visiting High Court judges could be particularly aggressive, usually in front of juries, but Gratton never allowed the judges to ruffle him. He was too nice for that, and, with his fine manner, backed by an edge of

steeliness, he put the judges in their place – politely, of course. That was Fern Gratton's way.

He developed his routines and rituals. He spent Friday nights in the office, readying for the following week in court and working straight through until Saturday morning, with time off only for a brief nap on the office couch. To keep his body in shape, he played volleyball every noon hour at the local Y, and to keep his rich baritone in tune, he sang every Sunday in the church choir. He was a conscientious delegator. Jean-Marc Labrosse, whose own career led him to an appointment to the Court of Appeal, articled with Gratton and found the training filled with so much personal responsibility that, when he was called to the bar, his own Sudbury practice was virtually set in place.

By the late 1950s, Gratton had become such a formidable opponent that the insurance company lawyers who travelled from Toronto to contest him in court were often inclined to throw up their hands in defeat. Gratton presented his case with detail that made it difficult for opposing counsel to raise so much as a question. The judges now looked on Gratton as clearly their favourite in the courtroom. And – the final blow for the insurers' lawyers – everybody on the juries seemed to be Gratton's good friend.

He proved an irresistibly likeable foe. He was a joker and a performer. He once wrote a hilariously ribald drama about a fellow Sudbury counsel, which the other lawyers in town performed with noisy relish at the stag before the counsel's wedding. Gratton's play brought the house down. He possessed a congeniality that was contagious, and he made a splendid host to visiting counsel at his cottage on Panage Lake – even as he planned to demolish his guests in the courtroom.

Gratton served on the Sudbury Separate School Board; he was the first French-speaking president of the city's Chamber of Commerce; and, on January 1, 1967, when he was just forty-one years old, he accepted an appointment to the Nipissing District Court in North Bay. At the time, the court list was in disarray, with a long backlog of cases, particularly on the criminal side. Gratton applied himself to the list and, in an astonishingly short period of time, it was tidy and up to date. Gratton soon became Nipissing's ideal judge, providing brisk hearings and well-crafted decisions.

In his career at the bar and on the bench, Fern Gratton was the man who got out the heavy fire only for hunting. He saved the fine touch, reflected in his writing and oratory, for the courtroom.

Bernard William Hurley (b. 1927)

As Ben Hurley often said of himself, he made two wise moves in his life: one was to marry his wife, and the other was to settle in Belleville, Ontario. The two moves went together.

Hurley's wife was born on a farm in Marysville, not far from Belleville, and the latter town struck Hurley, a native of Toronto, as a logical place to practise law. It turned out to be better than logical. As far as Hurley was concerned, Belleville was perfect.

Hurley grew up a Catholic kid in Toronto's east end. He attended St. Michael's College at the University of Toronto and then Osgoode Hall, where he received his call to the bar in 1950. In Belleville, which Hurley found ideal and welcoming from the start, he joined a firm that included three other lawyers; one of them was a remarkable counsel who had a lasting impact on the way Hurley handled himself in the courts. This counsel was Malcolm Robb, eleven years older than Hurley, a Second World War veteran and an advocate who was in the process of refining his courtroom technique. Robb practised for most of his career in Toronto, but he lived and worked in Belleville from 1947 to 1954, which was just long enough to teach young Ben Hurley a thing or two.

Robb went at trial preparation with acute precision, and in the courtroom he radiated conviction. These were attitudes and traits that Robb passed on to the willing Hurley. "When Malcolm wasn't satisfied with what I did in a case,"

Hurley said, "he had a direct way of making his dissatisfaction plain to me." So it was that the Hurley approach followed the Robb model.

Perhaps, ironically, Hurley never set out to become exclusively a litigator. As he frequently told his five children (two future lawyers among them), many of their university fees and school boarding costs were paid out of real estate deals. But over the years, as word of Hurley's committed and diligent style in the courts spread through the Belleville area, his practice gravitated to litigation of both the civil and the criminal variety. Belleville didn't have enough crime to keep a counsel occupied at anything close to full time.

Real property cases became a small specialty for Hurley. Toronto lawyers of his generation could put in a lifetime of practice without encountering a single case in real property law, but Hurley took nine or ten such cases a year. They were fundamental to life in rural Ontario: disputes over property lines, arguments about possession of land as opposed to paper title, fights centred on rights of way. Hurley developed a knack with the arcana of real property.

He discovered other ways in which a country counsel's practice differed from those of his city brothers. Even though Hurley conducted the array of cases familiar to any counsel – contested wills, matrimonial breakdowns, automotive claims, an amazing murder case that he won with a defence of automatism – he found that one major difference in practising in a corner of eastern Ontario lay in the regularity with which he went to court against the same small group of counsel. This fact of litigation life, unknown to most urban barristers, required a deft hand, a need for Hurley to learn the other counsels' tricks without revealing his own. In a pinch, when he stumbled into a tricky legal backwater, he phoned his mentor and friend, Malcolm Robb, who was always available with advice.

In 1976 Hurley went to the bench and remained happily there until the last possible moment. On his mandatory retirement at age seventy-five, he said with the mock grumpy humour that identified him, "I resented that I was turned out of a job I loved at high noon on April 18, 2002." In the following years he took mediation work, sat on the Pension Appeal Board, and reflected on the two wise moves of a half-century earlier that landed him in Belleville, the perfect place to practise law.

Julia Verlyn LaMarsh (1924–1980)

A suspected bank robber on the run from a holdup stole Judy LaMarsh's car. It was 1951, and LaMarsh had just entered her second year of practice in a partnership with her father in Niagara Falls.

When the police caught the car thief and alleged holdup man, LaMarsh stepped forward in her professional capacity to defend the man at his trial on the bank robbery charges. She won an acquittal. And she got back her car.

LaMarsh accomplished so much in so many fields – politics, government, communications – that her lively career as a courtroom lawyer is often overlooked. The LaMarsh partnership of father and daughter conducted a practice in the Falls area, where Mr. La-Marsh was for years the Stamford Township solicitor. When he died in 1957, his daughter succeeded him in the post, making Judy LaMarsh the first township solicitor of her sex in Canada. But no matter how busy she kept herself with solicitor's duties, LaMarsh made room for litigation. It was the courtroom, particularly the criminal courts, that most excited and motivated her.

She followed an indirect educational route to reach the law. After high school, she earned a primary school teaching certificate, but rather than teach, she joined the Canadian Women's Army Corps. It was 1943, the war was on, and LaMarsh found herself posted to the Royal Canadian Engineers in Halifax. Then she transferred across the country to Vancouver, where she studied Japanese on an army course. The language skill equipped her for an assignment in the United States as a translator of Japan's secret war documents. At the war's end, she took a Bachelor of Arts at the University of Toronto, entered Osgoode Hall, received her call

Judy LaMarsh and Lester B. Pearson

to the bar in 1950, and set up shop with her father.

In her criminal practice, LaMarsh never backed away from the most demanding cases. She defended in a dozen rape trials and in four murder cases. Of the latter, three trials ended in convictions for manslaughter. In the fourth trial, her client was convicted of first-degree murder, an occasion that brought on LaMarsh's one and only display of weeping in public. "I'm more inclined to use invective than tears," she said years later.

Her strong suits in the courtroom were her swift grasp of detail and what she described as her "habit of attack." These were qualities that translated naturally to the political life that took LaMarsh to Ottawa in 1960, as a Liberal member of parliament under Lester Pearson. She was appointed to cabinet in 1963. As minister of national health and welfare, she oversaw the new Canada Pension Plan, and, later as secretary of state, she was in charge of the vast and joyful celebrations that marked the country's Centennial Year.

Retired from politics in 1968, LaMarsh spread her talents wide. She wrote a controversial autobiography, *Memoirs of a Bird in a Gilded Cage*. She hosted radio programs for the CBC and for private broadcasters. She taught at Osgoode Hall Law School. She headed a royal commission inquiring into violence in the media. She wrote two novels. And for one last time, she returned to the criminal courtroom to conduct the defence in a case that, typical for LaMarsh, seemed perverse, comic, and meaningful.

At a 1974 amateur talent night in a popular Toronto bar named the Brunswick House, four young gay women performed a song they called "a dyke ditty." When the Brunswick House pulled the plug on the young women's act, the bar erupted in a mini-riot. Police charged the four women with creating a public disturbance, and LaMarsh took their case *pro bono*. By the time she finished applying her whirlwind defence tactics at the trial, charges had been withdrawn against one young woman, two others were acquitted, and only the fourth was convicted and sentenced to three months of probation. In LaMarsh fashion, she complained long and loud about the conviction, but the case was one that she talked of with pride until her death in 1980.

Phillip Barry Chaytor Pepper (1922–1997)

Barry Pepper had the appearance of a barrister in a 1940s English film. He was tall, with a slight slouch, dashing looks, and hair worn in a sweeping cut.

Barry Pepper and the Queen Mother at Campbell House, Toronto

In and out of court he spoke as if he were an actor delivering lines, gifted with the exquisite phrasing and timing of Gregory Peck in *The Parradine Case*. He liked to present his views of the profession in amusing axioms that he coined himself. "You can't play a case in high C all the way through," he said. It was Pepper's idiosyncratic way of saying a counsel need not maintain the same level of intensity during an entire trial.

If Pepper's speech and manner suggested Englishness, he came by it honestly. He was born in Lichfield, Staffordshire, and earned a degree from Brasenose College, Oxford. But his connections with Canada dated from fairly early in his life. He joined the RCAF during the Second World War and flew escort planes for ships in Atlantic convoys. After the war and after Oxford, when he married his Toronto bride, he made a permanent home on this side of the Atlantic, receiving his call in 1950 and commencing a distinguished career at the bar.

Two prominent counsel had their influences on Pepper in his early years. One was Joe Sedgwick, with whom Pepper served part of his articles, and the other was John Robinette, who hired Pepper as a freelance junior for a half-dozen cases. From Sedgwick, Pepper learned how to maintain aplomb in court and how to bring a touch of humour to the proceedings without slighting his serious regard for the law. In Robinette's company, Pepper absorbed the meaning of research,

of readying the case, and presenting it to the court with clarity and depth.

Following his call, Pepper spent a period in his own criminal practice, then joined McMillan, Binch for a stint in which he initiated the firm's litigation department. Next, he put together another small advocacy firm of his own, which lasted until 1966, when he signed on with Fraser, Beatty. He remained there for the rest of his career, shaping the firm's litigation practice into one of the finest in Toronto.

Pepper had a natural curiosity about all kinds of subjects. "I've always been interested in such things as how paper is made," he said. "How electricity works, how men dig mines. As it happened not by chance, all of those matters came up in cases I litigated." His inquisitiveness appeared to know no bounds; he took cases in admiralty and in combines, in medical malpractice, constitutional law, trade-marks and patents. He acted for a football team in a contract dispute with its former quarterback. He represented the captain of a wayward Great Lakes ship that knocked down the bridge over the Burlington Channel. And he argued a case in which the issue to be determined was whether the machine in question was legally a vacuum cleaner or a humidifier. The answer was vacuum cleaner, and Pepper won the argument.

If he had his choice, he preferred trial work because, in his words, "I enjoyed the stage management of it." But the preference didn't stop him from accepting appeal briefs of great scope and even greater complexity. Among them were more than fifty cases that he argued in full appeal before the Supreme Court of Canada.

Throughout his career, Pepper had a propensity for finding himself in bizarre circumstances in Ontario's courtrooms. That was what occurred in a 1962 trial in which he argued opposite Dick Holland before Mr. Justice Dalton Wells. The judge grew upset over a line of questioning that Holland put to a witness, and, in his distraction, Wells absentmindedly lit up a cigarette in court. As smoke swirled around Wells' oblivious head, Pepper rose languidly to his feet and said in an even voice: "If Your Lordship pleases, may we take a five-minute adjournment." Wells, suddenly shocked to find a burning cigarette in his hand, granted the request, hurried from the courtroom, and was forever grateful to the always cool, urbane, and sophisticated Barry Pepper.

Barry Pepper was president of The Advocates' Society from 1974 to 1976.

John Douglas Bowlby (1926–1989)

John Bowlby, a born storyteller, liked to repeat the one about a wayward moment in his youth.

One summer night, John and another teenager, equipped with BB guns, shot out the streetlights in the Lake Huron cottage town of Southampton. A local policeman nabbed the two boys and marched John in front of his father.

"Mr. Bowlby," the policeman declared, "your son will be either a great man or a terrible criminal."

The closest John Bowlby got to terrible criminals in later years was when he defended them in court. In fact, he followed a professional path not unlike that of his father, the man who founded the family's law firm in Hamilton, Ontario, and proceeded in due course to a place on the Court of Appeal. The junior Bowlby joined the firm in 1951, carved out a fine record as a counsel, and similarly ended his career on the bench.

He earned his early reputation in criminal work. Two other young lawyers named John were launched in a similar direction in Hamilton at the same time, John Agro and John White, and, with the passing years, the three Johns dominated the city's criminal bar. Bowlby acted for crooks accused of murdering cops and for cops suspected of exchanging favours with crooks. He became an omnipresent figure in Hamilton's criminal courts, and, with the refining of his courtroom technique, he soon put his hand to a wider span of litigation.

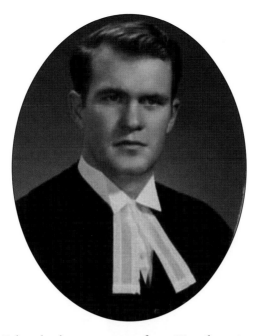

He represented John Munro, the Liberal cabinet minister from Hamilton, in a libel action against the *Toronto Sun*. The newspaper claimed that Munro had used his political influence to benefit from Petrocan's takeover of a chain of gas stations in Hamilton. When the *Sun*'s story disintegrated in court, Bowlby won damages for Munro of $70,000, the largest libel award in Ontario at the time.

Insurance companies retained Bowlby to defend lawsuits in the Hamilton area, and he made himself so adept in the field that claims managers at more than one company swore that plaintiffs trembled when John Bowlby strode into the courtroom. He was the Hamilton Harbour Commission's choice of counsel in its civil action against several dredging companies accused in a bid-rigging conspiracy. He represented the Hamilton multimillionaire Michael DeGroot in his contentious divorce from the first Mrs. DeGroot. And he acted for yet another Liberal cabinet minister in a libel case, this time negotiating a settlement when an Ottawa Crown attorney brought a suit against Jean Marchand.

Bowlby attacked every case with supreme gusto. Without resorting to arrogance or belligerence, he left no doubt of his presence in the courtroom, and he approached life outside the courts in the same large spirit. Bowlby was the sort of Irishman whose eyes filled with tears at the first bar of "Danny Boy." He loved a drink, a laugh, and a practical joke. He stood fast by his friends and his colleagues. "If I had a problem," said his long-time partner Fred Luchak, "John was the only guy I wanted at my side."

Bowlby was elected a bencher in 1966 and worked assiduously at his Law Society tasks. Among his fellow benchers, he gathered such support that he made a piece of history in 1980 by becoming the first bencher from outside Toronto to succeed to the office of treasurer. Typical of Bowlby, he showed his streak of contrariness by having his treasurer's portrait painted not by an Ontario artist, as was the custom, but by a Bowlby pal whose studio was in London, England, where the sittings took place in convivial circumstances. Everybody agreed that the resulting portrait caught the nature of the endlessly uproarious Bowlby.

In 1982 he received an appointment to the Ontario High Court, but his career on the bench was cut short by his early death.

John Francis Howard (b. 1924)

Towards the end of his career, Jake Howard's secretary gave him a present that he treasured. It was a framed copy of lawyers' hourly billing rates at Blake, Cassels & Graydon in 1953, the year Howard joined the firm.

Howard's rate was a lowly $3.45. He hung the document over his desk and never failed to laugh about it with visitors to his office. From the beginning, Howard was a man entirely without airs, a leading counsel who didn't take himself seriously, but took his clients' problems so seriously that he worked long, hard, and brilliantly on their behalf.

He was born in the Colombian town of Berranca Bermeja, where his father was employed by International Petroleum. As a child, Howard learned to speak Spanish as well as he spoke English, but he did most of his growing up after the family moved back to Toronto. He served for four years in the navy during the Second World War and, after the war, he worked his way through the University of Toronto, where he took a commerce degree, and through Osgoode Hall.

During his articles at Blake, Cassels, it was the renowned civil litigator Arthur Patillo who exerted a profound influence on Howard. "Arthur had a motto," Howard said. "'Get me the facts. The law will take care of itself.' That's what Arthur preached, and I came to believe the same thing in my own practice."

He had to bide his time at Blakes, since the firm observed a rule that required junior lawyers to spend a year in real estate and another year in the corporate department before they moved to litigation. "Watching Arthur in court was the

most important part of my education," Howard said, "because, that way, I learned how things were done properly."

In the decades that followed, Howard did things properly for a list of clients that included many of the most prestigious corporations in Canada. He successfully defended Imperial Oil in a combines prosecution of the fertilizer industry in the late 1970s, and he was similarly victorious in the defence of Southam Inc. in a monopoly prosecution in the early 1980s. He served as counsel for the Canadian Imperial Bank of Commerce, Ontario Hydro, and Global Television. He filled the roles of chief counsel to the McDonald Commission investigating Canada's Security Service, and of counsel to Magna Inc. and Frank Stronach at the Parker Royal Commission into the activities of cabinet minister Sinclair Stevens.

Perhaps his favourite case in a career that touched all the bases came in the mid-1970s, when he represented the minority shareholders of the Ontario and Quebec Railway against the Canadian Pacific Railway. The CPR had obtained from the O and Q a perpetual lease of all its lands running from Montreal to Windsor. Unnoticed by shareholders, the CPR was selling off the lands and, at the same time, buying up O and Q stock. The shareholders sued.

"That case was humungous," Howard recalled with pleasure. "We needed to prove a mountain of facts. But we succeeded."

What particularly tickled Howard was the discovery among the CPR records of a sale of 50 acres of former O and Q land near Bethany, Ontario, to none other than John Francis Howard. Though he hadn't known the land's previous history, these acres made up the first piece of country property where Howard began his love affair with horses – the passion of his life away from the law.

At first, on the Bethany property and then at a larger farm northwest of Toronto, Howard and the rest of his family were satisfied simply by riding horses. But eventually he took the next step and put together an impressive stable of racehorses. Just as he relished the digging for facts that was necessary to his brand of litigation, he brought enthusiasm to the building of a winning stable, one that included such champions as Mordacious, the winner of four stake races. Howard became a leader in the track world, serving as chairman of the Jockey Club, in the same manner as he had already made himself a leader at the bar.

Alfred Anthony Petrone (b. 1925)

Alf Petrone brought a sleeping bag packed with 117 kilos of potatoes into court. He proposed to make the potatoes an exhibit in his defence of a client facing a charge of first-degree murder.

In order to have completed the crime, the accused would have had to hoist the murdered man's body into a freezer. Petrone's point was that his client, a slight fellow, wasn't capable of the lifting job on his own. Since the body weighed 117 kilos, Petrone came up with the notion of the potato-filled sleeping bag. After much argument, the judge threw the potatoes out of the courtroom. Petrone still managed to win a reduced conviction for his client.

The potatoes were vintage Petrone. In his long and celebrated career as the top gun among criminal lawyers in northwestern Ontario, he proved himself to be a counsel with a big bag of tricks. A naturally ebullient man, Petrone threw every element of his effervescent personality into the defence of his clients. He was flexible enough to mute his approach when subtlety was called for, but it was his passionate moments that most electrified Thunder Bay's courtrooms.

"You're getting too emotional, Mr. Petrone," Justice William Maloney once warned him in court.

"You're the one who's MAKING me emotional!" Petrone fired back.

Maloney was hardly surprised at Petrone's reaction. The two men had been Osgoode Hall classmates and fellow coun-

sel in the Lakehead, and it was Maloney who once characterized Petrone as resilient, resourceful, and utterly irrepressible.

Petrone grew up in the north, the son of Italian immigrants, and, by his mid-teens, he was working in the construction business. He joined the Canadian Navy during the Second World War, and, when he returned to civilian life, he rethought his future. He completed his high school classes, received an undergraduate degree from the University of Western Ontario, and graduated in the Osgoode Hall class of 1953.

His first murder case came a year later, after Petrone had set up his one-man practice in Port Arthur. As a first case, it was a heartbreaker. Petrone's client was charged with shooting his own son to death, and, before the case reached an end, Petrone had seen it through two trials, two convictions, two appeals, and a rare hearing in the accused man's native country of Finland. Despite Petrone's heroic efforts, his client was sentenced to be hanged and received a cabinet reprieve only on the day of the scheduled execution.

Rather than discourage Petrone from murder trials, the drama of this first case had the effect of committing him to a lifetime as defence counsel in the most horrible of the Lakehead's killings. He took more than fifty murder trials; a remarkable seven of them were cases in which the accused was a woman. Petrone and the firm he built, Petrone Hornak Garofalo Maure, became noted for an industrious and able civil litigation practice, but Petrone established his greatest reputation in criminal law.

He was indefatigable in defence of clients. For thirty years he employed an assistant, Frances Duffield, who sleuthed relentlessly on her boss's murder cases, playing Della Street to Petrone's Perry Mason. In one case a client on a murder charge claimed he hadn't shot at the victim. His story was that he fired only at the floor, intending it as a shot of warning, and the bullet accidentally ricocheted into the victim. Duffield and Petrone searched the murder scene for hours until they found the groove in the floor from the flying bullet. Petrone used the evidence to beat the first-degree murder charge.

In the fervour of his defences, Petrone could exasperate the court. Twice, judges cited him for contempt, once as the result of a quarrel with the judge about the configurations of a table. Was it round or square? Petrone lost the quarrel, though both contempt citations were later purged. Petrone was a counsel who kept himself primed for argument at all times, even when the subject of debate was a bag of potatoes.

Donald Finlay Sim (1927–1986)

Don Sim had a propensity for acting on the spur of the moment. That was what he did in a courtroom on a day in the late 1970s when he was arguing a case that concerned the patent on a brand of door frame.

Intellectual property was Sim's field, one in which he was rivalled at his peak only by Gordon Henderson of Ottawa. In the door-frame case, Sim set out to make the point before the trial judge that the frame in question was uniquely strong and singularly effective. He placed the frame on the floor of the courtroom and, to demonstrate its strength and effectiveness, he stood on the frame. Sim was a big man, six-and-a-half feet tall, weighing close to three hundred pounds, and, under his formidable bulk, the door frame broke with a resounding crack.

At this embarrassing turn of events, other counsel might have fallen into an aghast silence. Not Sim.

"And look, my Lord," he said to the judge, "look at how symmetrically this remarkable door frame has broken."

For all his considerable size, Sim was fast on his feet, both physically and metaphorically. Few counsel could match him for speed in arriving at a point in a courtroom exchange. He thought two or three steps ahead in whatever train of argument he pursued. He enjoyed the thrill of spontaneity in a trial or on an appeal, but he always had a firm grasp on his ultimate destination. Quick thinking was his great strength.

Sim grew up in Kitchener, Ontario, a Baptist and a Scot, the son of a one-time Canadian trade commissioner to Scot-

land. In his mid-teens, he joined the Canadian Merchant Marine. The Second World War was almost over, and Sim said he just wanted to get in on the party that would celebrate the Allied victory. After the celebration, he took a degree in mechanical engineering at Queen's University, attended Osgoode Hall, and received his call to the bar in 1953.

Sim articled with Harold Fox, a specialist in trade-mark, patent, and copyright law, and he joined Fox in practice at McCarthy & McCarthy, where Fox was a counsel. The two remained there until 1969, when they left to form their own firm, which continued into the twenty-first century as two firms, Sim Hughes and Sim & McBurney. Throughout his career, Sim confined himself to intellectual property, a field in which he soon came to excel.

He represented the Ford Motor Company, Union Carbide, and other major clients in disputes over copyrights and trade-marks. He was first choice among many leading law firms that needed to retain outside counsel on tricky cases involving aspects of intellectual property. And inevitably, in the old Exchequer Court or in Federal Court, he often found himself arguing against Gordon Henderson. These were exhilarating occasions, bristling with the two men's competitive spirit, mixing a dash of show business with the collision of legal argument. The exchanges served to sharpen the talents of both counsel. Sim, for his part, never felt overmatched.

He commanded the courtroom with a largeness of spirit that matched his imposing physical presence. On one case before President Jackett of the Exchequer Court, Sim described an argument from Henderson as an example of his point that "all these people from big firms think like that." Jackett shot back, "Mr. Sim, you're a big firm all by yourself."

Sim was a social creature, a friendly man who led an active life as a skier and a tennis player, and it came as a shock when he died suddenly at age fifty-eight in 1986. His partner Roger Hughes, delivering the eulogy at the funeral, ended with a reference to Sim's character as a people person. Hughes told of one occasion when, leaving Sim's office, he asked whether Sim wanted the door closed.

"Don't ever shut the door, Roger," Sim answered. "You never know when a nice person might come by and say hello."

Pierre Genest (1930–1989)

Born in Ottawa, Pierre Genest learned the notion of service to his profession and his country from the examples set by his own family.

Genest's grandfather campaigned vigorously as a champion of French Canadian rights, and his father capped a distinguished life in the law on the Supreme Court of Ontario. With Pierre's call to the bar in 1954, he put himself on the same path of duty set by the two senior Genests.

Early in his career he came under the mentorship of the leading Toronto counsel, David Griffiths, and it was after both men joined the Cassels Brock firm that Genest spread his wings in civil litigation. A pivotal point in his advocacy occurred in 1972 at the provincial inquiry into the construction of the Ontario Hydro building. Genest represented the building's contractor with such intelligence and verve that, from then on, he was in constant demand as a counsel, his desk overflowing with major briefs.

His strength as an advocate lay in his facility with language. He was a superb draftsman and was equally adept on his feet in a courtroom, an articulate spokesman for his cause – succinct, committed, and able to freshen any proceeding with a dash of welcome humour. What he possessed, in the words of his friend and partner John DesBrisay, was "a capacity to distil the complex so as to make it simple and to present the simple with artistry."

In the mid-1970s he brought this artistry to a claim by a Dutch resident against a significant store of CPR shares. What delighted Genest was that the claim dated from 1915, making it the most ancient case ever to make its way through Canadian courts. The First World War had initially stalled the case, and then it had wandered in the judicial wilderness until a Statement of Claim was issued in the 1930s, only to be halted again by the Second World War. When Genest got his hands on the brief, he took discovery of the original broker on the 1915 deal, a man in his nineties by the time of the examination. With the broker's testimony, Genest won at trial and on appeal, bringing to an end a case that was six decades old and providing him with the sort of colourful story from the courts that he loved to tell.

In his family's tradition, Genest served the federal government in countless roles. He argued the federal cause in the Manitoba French-language constitutional issue. He sat as a commissioner on the Northwest Territories Council and rewrote the Territories legislation. He was senior adviser to Minister of Justice Jean Chrétien in 1980 and 1981 at the time Chrétien was grappling with the development of the *Charter of Rights*. He acted for Ontario Hydro during a tricky moment when he had to announce to the public that hydro rates were about to rise. And he handled the even more delicate job of carrying out a federal inquiry into whether the American CIA had infiltrated Canada's security system and financed Quebec's separatist movement.

By the mid-1980s Genest was at the zenith of his health, power, and influence. He appeared regularly in the Court of Appeal and the Supreme Court of Canada. He sat on the boards of such companies as Power Corporation and Suncor. He was elected treasurer of the Law Society in the spring of 1985. And he led an active physical life – a skier, a golfer, a tennis player, a man who competed ferociously at every game he took up.

Then, in December 1985, he suffered a severe stroke. His lifestyle necessarily changed, but his intellect refused to surrender. In November 1987, when a group of partners at Cassels Brock put into action their plan to leave and form a new firm, there was no question that Genest would accompany them. Even suffering from the stroke's disabilities, Genest remained a leader, a counsel of much wisdom and a man with a talent for friendship. It was his name that appeared first in the name of the new firm, and, years after his death in the spring of 1989, his name has stayed in place at Genest Murray.

Elmer Walter Sopha (1924–1982)

When word got around the halls of the Ontario legislature that Elmer Sopha was rising to speak in the House, everyone in the building flocked to the chamber.

Sopha sat as Sudbury's Liberal MPP from 1957 to 1971, and he reigned as the legislature's resident spellbinder. He was caustic, witty, audacious, and smart, and he fired at a wide range of targets: the monarchy, the prayer before daily sittings of the House, Ontario's flag, breweries, the office of the lieutenant-governor, and the bounty on wolves. Wolves were a recurring theme with Sopha. He took their side against the hunters.

Sopha brought the same unorthodoxy and jovial eloquence to his practice in the courts. Born in Cobalt in northern Ontario, the son of a miner, Sopha was late arriving in the profession. First he served in the navy for six years during the Second World War, then attended the University of Toronto and Osgoode Hall. He received his call to the bar in 1955 at age thirty-one, which was when he set out to make up for lost time, practising litigation law in Sudbury.

Sopha loved to put on a show in the courtroom. He could roll out the orotund phrases with the best of them, snipe at opponents with grand insults, upbraid judges while never seeming less than a gentleman. But Sopha knew how to take matters a step deeper into performance. In one case that was going to ruin for him in Sudbury's old Magistrate's Court, he finally turned his back on the recalcitrant magistrate and addressed a fifteen-minute summation of the case for his client to the crowd of spectators in the courtroom. Sopha failed to save the client from conviction, but he was damned if he wouldn't put on a show.

Behind Sopha's theatrics, a fine legal mind was at work. It began with a prodigious memory. Ted Conrad, Sopha's partner for fourteen years, was astounded at the lack of paper in the files that Sopha kept of his cases, sometimes not a single sheet. It was all in Sopha's head – the facts, the witness list, the argument. He could read forty pages of intricate medical material, pick out the six or seven lines relevant to his case, commit them to memory, and submit a doctor to an hour of cross-examination without a note in sight. Sopha in court was as adept as a conjurer on stage.

He was intensely devoted to Sudbury, its reputation and its environment. He conducted lawsuits that protected the region in uranium exploration by Hollinger Mines, and he jumped all over a proposal that American astronauts should train in Sudbury because the area resembled the lunar landscape. But Sopha's scope in outlook and learning took him far wider than the geographical area he championed and the profession he practised. In the true sense of the words, he was a cultured man.

Service in the Canadian Navy took Sopha around the world the first time, and he kept on repeating the experience on his own for the rest of his life. As a counsel, he worked day and night for three months on his caseload, then took a break in Guatemala or Austria or Morocco. This was the routine of his life, one that sometimes led to awkwardness for Conrad and others in the office who had to cover for Sopha in court. But his enormous curiosity about the world kept him on the move.

Besides, it was Sopha's view that exposure to different cultures made him better and more adaptive in his roles as a counsel and a legislator. If some of his positions seemed quirky, even daffy – he favoured, for instance, a change in the costumes worn by judges and counsel because he said the gowns made them resemble Batman and contributed an unnecessary sense of mystery to the law – they were actually the considered views of a serious man. It was altogether typical of the deeper Sopha that, at his death, he was working on a biography of Mr. Justice Riddell, of the Ontario Supreme Court, whom he felt history had overlooked. Being overlooked was never a personal problem for Elmer Sopha.

Douglas Kerr Laidlaw (1928–1984)

The lawsuit would turn on Doug Laidlaw's examination for discovery of the nuclear scientist. Laidlaw's client was an engineering contractor who had designed a heavy water plant in Nova Scotia.

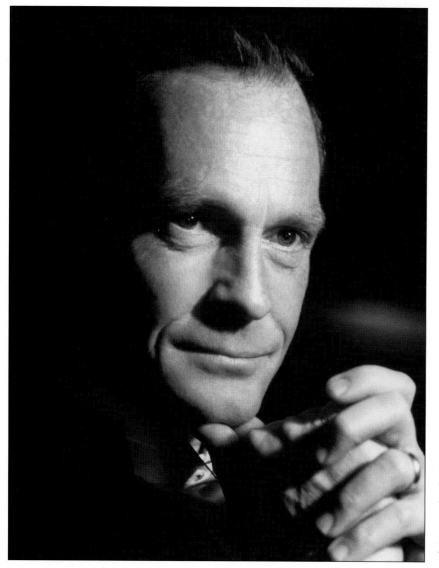

The plant failed to work, and the government of Nova Scotia sued the contractor. Hundreds of millions of dollars were at stake. The plaintiff's principal witness was a nuclear scientist – the last remaining employee of the plant and an expert in his complex field. Laidlaw's junior, Ron Slaght, devoted weeks to getting a handle on the technology of heavy water. For the three days before the discovery, Slaght briefed Laidlaw. Then, over two days, Laidlaw engaged the nuclear scientist. The questioning covered the scientist's own turf, yet Laidlaw, who had made himself entirely conversant with the minutiae of heavy water science, won breathtaking admissions from the scientist. There were admissions that absolved the contractor's design from blame for the plant's failure. It was a sublime performance, a textbook example of the art of discovery, something that Slaght decided he would never see equalled by another counsel.

Doug Laidlaw was a consummate barrister, possessing all the tools: vitality, searching intellect, a voice with a timbre that seized attention, and the ability to absorb complicated concepts and give them back in persuasive language in the courtroom. He had a

particular knack for arriving at what he determined to be the issue in a given case and compelling the court to agree that, yes, this really was the only issue worth considering. Laidlaw had aggression to burn, and, though he always made clear his respect for the court, especially for the Supreme Court of Canada (he was second only to John Robinette in his number of appearances before it), he never suffered fools, even if they happened to sit on that court. When Justice Louis-Philippe Pigeon asked him the same question three times in the course of a Supreme Court appeal, Laidlaw said: "My Lord, I've answered that question twice. I'm going to answer it once more, but it's the last time, so pay attention." Not a word of rebuke came from the panel of nine justices.

Laidlaw's father, Robert, was a brilliant lawyer whose career took him to the Court of Appeal, and young Doug grew up in traditional upper-middle-class Toronto circumstances. But in university he had a brief and bizarre episode of dropping out. He decamped for the United States, where he sold women's hosiery door to door, relying on a patter that he could deliver by rote years later. Returning to Toronto, he received his call to the bar in 1956 and joined McCarthy & McCarthy. Within a couple of weeks of his arrival, Robinette sent him off to conduct a murder trial. For the next three decades, Laidlaw hardly raised his head from his work, moving through one case to the next in the manner of the constantly engaged counsel.

He was fanatically loyal to his clients, who made up an eclectic collection. He summoned equal passion in defence of doctor members of the Canadian Medical Practice Association who were sued for malpractice and of Xaviera Hollander, popularly known as the Happy Hooker, whom Canada's immigration officials sought to deport. He successfully defended the potash industry against Saskatchewan's effort to nationalize it; he won an acquittal for a Vancouver businessman charged in the Hamilton Harbour dredging case; and, on behalf of Peter Pocklington, he fended off a psychic who claimed a percentage of Pocklington's investment profits.

Laidlaw was disarming and unpretentious, a man who never seemed to notice that he had dressed himself in socks and tie that had no relation in colour or style to his suit – which was, in any event, more likely than not made of polyester. He rushed at life with vigour and curiosity. He played squash with his juniors at the end of a day in court. He skied in winter, sailed in summer. When his wife gave him gliding lessons for his fiftieth birthday, he announced with typical enthusiasm that it was the best of all sports. On the day of his sudden and tragic death a few years later, he was headed for yet a few more hours of gliding, a man intent on action to the end.

William Bruce Affleck (1930–1996)

Bruce Affleck used to say he was the best Crown attorney in Canada. He didn't doubt his status for a minute. "I've also got a photographic memory," he added. "And my IQ is 149. That's genius level."

Affleck's self-regard was large and puncture proof. But he was a likeable egotist, a big man with an open face, a frank manner, and a limitless fund of good cheer. Nobody minded when he made extravagant boasts for himself. Besides, he may have been right about his claim to be the best.

Affleck grew up in Oshawa, the son of a General Motors worker. He paid his way through the University of Toronto by working as a nightclub bouncer. Called to the bar in 1957, he spent three years in private practice, then joined the Crown's office in his hometown. He was thirty years old, the youngest Crown attorney in the country at the time, and on his way, he announced, to becoming better than all the rest.

Over the following seventeen years, Affleck prosecuted forty-five murder cases and survived three heart attacks. He tackled his case list each day with speed and an affection for brevity. He had a knack for condensing to the critical detail. If the police gave him one hundred witnesses for a big trial, Affleck called just twenty-five of them. He kept the facts and the law short and simple for the jury. He avoided legal jargon and never allowed a Latin term to cross his lips. He didn't say *mens rea* but, rather, "state

of mind." As Affleck put it, "If I talked about *mens rea* in an Oshawa courtroom, the jurors would call their doctors to see whether they had a dose of it."

He worked the courts the way an old standup comic played the Copacabana. He tossed off asides; he needled defence counsel; and he didn't hesitate to step all over the judge's lines. But Affleck's show-biz approach was backed up by his unflagging devotion to the Crown's job of presenting sound cases against the accused. He knew his law, and he could quote precedent from that photographic memory of his. One particular mastery was cross-examining medical witnesses. He was quick to withdraw a case if he considered the available evidence insufficient to get a conviction, a custom that contributed to his high rate of cases won. But most of Affleck's success was built on the grinding work of preparation – a dedication to duty that was reflected, alas, in the three heart attacks.

His most famous convictions came in the trial of the Great Windsor Bank Robbery of December 18, 1971. Six masked and armed robbers swept into a Royal Bank branch in Windsor, Ontario, and left after eleven minutes with more than a million dollars in cash. Later, police recovered a trunk packed with $155,000 of the loot. They charged six professional stickup men with the crime, and Affleck was parachuted in from Oshawa to conduct the prosecution. The six accused hired top counsel and produced confident alibis. But over the course of the ten-week trial, Affleck attacked on two fronts: he connected the men to the recovered money, and he broke down their alibis. In a bravura performance, consistently cutting off the defence at the pass, he won convictions and twenty-year sentences for five of the six men charged in the biggest bank robbery in Canadian history.

On November 1, 1977, Affleck retired from the Crown's office, an event marked by a farewell banquet that 112 lawyers and eight judges happily attended. Affleck opened an Oshawa criminal practice and prospered. Men he had once put away as a Crown attorney, members of biker gangs in particular, retained him because they remembered how adroitly Affleck had prosecuted them. Though he flourished in his new role, Affleck regarded defence work as duck soup compared to the tough slogging of the Crown's life. And he missed the glamour of his old job, the one at which he shone in the legal world.

"As a Crown," Affleck said, "you're always at centre stage."

Louis Henry Tepper (b. 1930)

When Lou Tepper was just six years old, he experienced a childhood epiphany. It came on a day when his father took him on one of his business trips into downtown Kingston, Ontario.

Mr. Tepper worked in the auto-parts industry in the town, and, for the business call, he led little Lou into an office in one of Kingston's handsome nineteenth-century buildings. There, as the boy listened in enthralled silence, his father talked of deals and arrangements with a man who sat back with his feet up on his desk. The man's confidence and assurance impressed young Lou, and so did the fact that his father paid money to this pleasantly formidable gentleman. When father and son left the office, Lou asked his dad who the man was. "He's my lawyer," the father answered, and Tepper promptly piped up, "That's what I'm going to be when I grow up."

True to his declaration, Tepper took his Bachelor of Arts at Queen's University and an LL.B. at the University of Toronto, received his call to the bar in 1957, and returned to Kingston to set up a one-man litigation practice. He chose Kingston because he was a known quantity in the town. He decided on a sole practice because he wanted to be his own boss. And he focused on litigation because he thought it had an allure of glory about it and would provide a life of fascination.

In the first months of his new practice, a major legal aid case came through the door. The client was a farmhand charged with the capital murder of the farmer he worked

In all the rest of his years in practice, he never turned down a criminal client. He defended people who were headed for the Kingston Penitentiary and people who were already sentenced to the Pen. He even acted for guards at the institution.

for. The trouble had started when the farmer beat and punched his employee for not getting up early enough. Reeling from the beating, the farmhand staggered into the hut where he slept, came out with his .22, and shot the farmer dead. Tepper's break in the case came with the discovery by his wife, Geraldine, a law student at the time, of photographs that the police had failed to turn over to the defence. The photos, taken immediately after the farmhand's arrest, showed the horrific results of his beating from the farmer. Tepper played up the photos with the jury and was rewarded with a manslaughter verdict. The result was a sensation in Kingston but failed to make the headlines of the local newspaper, the *Whig-Standard*, because the Russians sent up *Sputnik* on the same day.

Despite *Sputnik*, Tepper's career was off with a rush. In all the rest of his years in practice, he never turned down a criminal client. He defended people who were headed for the Kingston Penitentiary and people who were already sentenced to the Pen. He even acted for guards at the institution. One guard, charged with smuggling drugs to an inmate, showed up on the first day of his trial with a picture he had painted of the *Last Supper*. He thought no jury would believe that the artist of such a painting could be capable of smuggling drugs. Tepper persuaded his client to keep the painting out of sight and proceeded to win an acquittal without benefit of the *Last Supper*.

He kept himself as active on the civil side as the criminal. He acted in car accidents galore, for both plaintiffs and insurance companies. He handled much divorce work, and, in the last ten years of his practice, he maintained an industrious sideline in representing lawyers who were sued for negligence. Litigation was his life and, as he had anticipated, he felt its glory.

He attributed his success in the courts to his tenacity – a counsel who bit his teeth into a case and never let go. But his unforgettable voice was what helped to win over many judges and juries. The Tepper voice was deep, rich, and easy, producing a persuasive sound not unlike that of announcers on middle-of-the-road radio stations. The voice's timbre got him an offer of a job in radio (he turned it down), and it was what first attracted his wife when she was a University of Toronto undergraduate (he didn't turn her down). And it was a contributing factor to the grand courtroom triumphs during his career as a counsel that he had first glimpsed in the epiphany of his six-year-old self.

Ronald Joseph Rolls (b. 1932)

On a working day in 1976, an older woman arrived by appointment to consult Ron Rolls on an estate matter. She came from a small Ontario town and had been referred to Rolls by a local lawyer.

She took an hour to describe her problem. It seemed that the woman's husband had died, and she was convinced that the trust company charged with administering his estate was mismanaging the assets. As she talked, Rolls' student took notes while Rolls sat nodding encouragement to the women, asking the occasional question but recording nothing on paper himself. When the woman left, Rolls called briskly for his secretary, the aptly named Sally Case, and proceeded to dictate to Miss Case what his student came to recognize as the perfect demand letter to the miscreants on the other side. Rolls referred not once to the student's notes. The problem and its solution had already been committed to Rolls' phenomenal memory, and it emerged in his dictation in a flow of precise paragraphs. When the matter proceeded to litigation some time later, Rolls succeeded in delivering to the woman exactly what he had promised her and exactly what he had demanded from the trust company in his original letter.

Precision was Ron Rolls' middle name. It entered into every aspect of his practice as a civil litigator, from his appearance to his presentation. He wore immaculate suits, shirts with French cuffs, a smart tie, and he never walked around the office in casual shirt sleeves. He spoke in complete paragraphs even when he wasn't dictating. He brought to each of his briefs a form of analysis that went straight to the

point. There was no room in his life or his practice for wasted motion or sloppy thinking. He was exact and correct in all things, and he adhered to the oldest traditions of his profession. He cringed at the sight of barristers strolling up Bay Street in their gowns. To Rolls, ever the traditionalist, gowns were not to be worn outside the precincts of the court.

Rolls grew up in Hamilton and spent his first articling year with the Evans firm of that city. For his second year of articles, he was taken at the Fasken firm, which he was invited to join after his call in 1958 and where he stayed for the rest of his working life. His bond was with the firm's principal litigator, Walter Williston. It seemed an unlikely combination in style, since Williston was Mr. Informal and Rolls was Mr. By the Book. But the two joined to make contributions of far-reaching value to the profession, both in and out of the courtroom. Together they wrote a definitive two-volume text on civil procedure, and both taught the subject at the Bar Admission course. Rolls invariably ended his last lecture of each session with a line directed at students who were anxious for hints on examination questions. "I hope," he said before sweeping dramatically out of the lecture room, "each of you gets what you deserve."

In court, Rolls tried a wide range of cases. Procedural matters were his forte, and he took much commercial litigation. He was far better arguing to judges than addressing juries, where his formality sometimes failed to register. Nevertheless, Rolls found himself daunted by nothing in his practice. He welcomed each new brief and attacked it with great relish. For all his proper ways, Rolls celebrated the process of litigation, and his final instruction to the dozens of juniors and students who came under his guidance was heartfelt. "Be sure to have fun," Rolls always told them. Then he would add, "And if you're not having fun, tell me and I'll fix it."

Ian Gilmour Scott (b. 1934)

On the morning of June 26, 1985, Ian Scott argued a case in the Ontario Court of Appeal. He won.

That afternoon, Lieutenant-Governor John Black Aird swore him in as the province's new attorney general in Premier David Peterson's recently formed Liberal government. In the evening of this day when Scott moved from private practice to public service, he went to a chic restaurant, where he lingered late with friends over banter, laughs, and a good wine.

It was a typical day in Scott's always crowded life, bursting with the three passions that drove him: the courtroom, politics, and a damn good social time. He decided early in his career that he wanted to make a difference with the talents that blessed him. As a counsel, he chose cases that seemed to him to represent a worthy cause or to raise a significant issue. And as attorney general, he initiated legislation that steered the province's legal apparatus in directions he deemed fresh and beneficial.

He worked hard in all his roles, taking time to smell the flowers. He loved gardening, opera, and movies. Alas, he also loved a cigarette – a three-pack-a-day smoker when he was under the stress of a complex appeal or a grinding political issue. He wasn't a man who took the moderate path in pursuit of anything that caught his enthusiasm.

Born in Ottawa into a family of lawyers, Scott had a disputatious nature, a steel-trap memory, and such single-minded determination that he overcame a troublesome stutter. But, graduating in the middle of the pack from Osgoode Hall Law School and receiving no bids for his services, he submitted applications to fifty law firms. As he often joked in later years, just one of the fifty replied. The exception was the Cameron, Brewin firm, and it was under Andy Brewin that Scott learned to flourish as a counsel.

Very early in Scott's time at the firm, Brewin sprung him loose with no advance warning on a tricky motion before Mr. Justice Wishart Spence. The Brewin firm represented a motel whose business was suffering from the operations of

a nearby twenty-four-hour fuel stop for trucks. The motel wanted the stop's hours restricted. When the neophyte Scott presented the case, Spence ruled in his favour. The truck stop appealed. The masterful Walter Williston appeared for the appellant opposite Scott in the Court of Appeal. The court came down on Scott's side. Still two years short of thirty, his litigation career was launched.

Scott developed into an articulate all-rounder, comfortable at trial, on appeal, and in front of administrative boards, a natural at laying on charm and humour before every forum. In the 1970s he served as counsel for the commissions inquiring into the riots at the Kingston Penitentiary; the funding of legal clinics in Ontario; and, most memorably, the historic Berger Inquiry into the proposed pipeline through the Mackenzie Valley.

Scott's calendar overflowed with obligations, a schedule that included lecturing in civil procedure at the University of Toronto Law School for seventeen years. He was given to double and triple booking, arguing an appeal in one court while trials or motions in which he was also counsel got under way in other courts. His juniors accepted it as a matter of course that their principal would often require bailing out. He was a man in perpetual motion. Even on the Berger Inquiry, he absented himself from the hearings for two weeks while he fulfilled another commitment to defend a Toronto man on a murder charge. The jury acquitted Scott's client.

As attorney general, he engineered controversial changes to the legal profession and the judiciary. He sought to end the awarding of QCs in Ontario, and he restructured the court system, amalgamating the district, county, and high courts into the General Division and placing Provincial Court judges on the same footing with Division Court judges. Scott shrugged off criticisms; one quality he never lacked was confidence.

When he stepped down from politics in 1992, he had barely resumed his practice when strokes deprived him of much of his speech and his capacity to read. Nevertheless, he produced a brave and enlightening autobiography in which he discussed every aspect of his professional and personal life. With his book, as with his career, Scott revealed himself to be a man of wit, stubbornness, and exuberance.

John Sopinka (1933–1997)

At the ceremony in May 1988 when John Sopinka was sworn in as a justice of the Supreme Court of Canada, he spoke to the gathering about his parents.

The two elder Sopinkas had immigrated to Canada from Ukraine in the 1920s, settling first in Saskatchewan, where Mr. Sopinka worked a farm through the Depression, then moving east to Hamilton, Ontario, where he found a job with International Harvester. It was a life of unremitting toil for both father and mother, one in which Mrs. Sopinka never learned to read or write in either Ukrainian or English. And yet, in the span of just a single generation, these two brave and determined people raised a son who came to serve on the highest court of their adopted country.

That was only part of the remarkable John Sopinka story. At age fifteen he played violin in the Hamilton Philharmonic Orchestra; later, while he practised law, he continued in the string sections of the Etobicoke Philharmonic and the Oakville Symphony. To finance his way through law school at the University of Toronto, he played professional football as a defensive backfielder for the Toronto Argos and the Montreal Alouettes. Musician, athlete, scholar: if any lawyer could be legitimately called a Renaissance man, it was Sopinka.

At law school he often attended Magistrate's Court, offering to act for people charged with traffic offences. He introduced himself in court as an *amicus curiae* and used the principles he had picked up in first-year criminal law to defend his clients. Sopinka wanted to get the feel of standing on his feet in a courtroom, because it was his plan from the beginning to specialize in litigation.

He articled under Walter Williston at the Fasken firm, and, after his call to the bar in 1960, he stayed on for a few years

as Williston's junior. Williston set a hard and unrelenting pace in both work and play. But Sopinka had no trouble keeping up with his senior, and it was under Williston that he began to shape his own approach to litigation. It was an approach based on tireless preparation. "The idea," Sopinka explained, "was to chase down every possible lead in a case, to go after every avenue of inquiry in search of evidence. The second idea behind the first idea was never to be caught by surprise, but possibly to catch the other side with something unexpected."

First with the Fasken firm and later with Stikeman, Elliott, Sopinka took on cases of every conceivable stripe. He defended the CBC in a libel action, and he served as counsel for the Ontario Human Rights Commission. He represented the Aga Khan, and he acted for the Northwest Territories at the Meech Lake constitutional accord. He made himself a familiar presence at the most prominent commissions of inquiry of his time: one that investigated aviation safety, another that looked into bank failures, a third that examined RCMP activities, and a fourth that delved into the dealings of the cabinet minister Sinclair Stevens.

It was in connection with yet another commission that Sopinka provided the service that he called the most satisfying in his career as a lawyer. The commission was under the direction of Mr. Justice Samuel Grange, whose task was to inquire into the mysterious deaths of babies at the Hospital for Sick Children. Sopinka's client was Susan Nelles, the young nurse who was at one point charged with responsibility for the deaths. Sopinka believed in Nelles' innocence. He fought for her with intellect and vigour, and, in the end, when all the proceedings were completed, Nelles was vindicated. From then on, in a demonstration of the respect and affection Sopinka generated in others, Nelles and her family remained friends to the end with Sopinka and his family.

Sopinka made a formidable opponent for other counsel. He brought to his cases a fine mind; he wrote books on concepts of evidence and of appeal work. And he was unyielding in the courtroom. "I'm always nervous before I go to court, just as I was nervous before a football game," he said. "But I've never felt intimidated, not in football games and not in courtrooms."

Not long after he joined the Supreme Court of Canada, appointed directly from private practice, he became one of the court's leaders. It wasn't a role he assumed through force of personality. Rather, as one of his colleagues expressed it, the leadership evolved because Sopinka's opinions were invariably well thought out and objectively framed. Nothing less was to be expected from the Renaissance man of Canadian law.

Paul Stephen Andrew Lamek (1936–2001)

It came as no real surprise to his fellow counsel when they discovered that Paul Lamek happened to be an excellent amateur actor. In and out of court, he was a man who relished flair and style.

As a litigator, his presentations drew success from the incisiveness of their language and the polish of their delivery. In the theatre, among other accomplishments, he gave a superb reading to the role of Captain Queeq in a 1993 production of *The Caine Mutiny Court Martial* staged by The Advocates' Society and the Canadian Stage Company. The two sides of Lamek, counsel and actor, were all of a piece for a man who loved the proper use of the well-spoken word.

Born in Blackpool, England, Lamek took his education, which included a law degree, at Oxford. He moved to the University of Pennsylvania on a teaching fellowship, but when the United States toughened its immigration laws, placing stringent requirements on those who were foreign born and held student visas, Lamek chose Toronto as his next destination. There he established a splendid career and a full life.

The career began with five years of lecturing at Osgoode Hall Law School, 1962 to 1967, a period when he emerged as an influential teacher of the law. He was knowledgeable, he was eloquent, and he possessed a talent for conveying a true sense of the meaning of the rule of law. This combination of talents made him an inspiration to Osgoode students of the time. As one of the students, Harvey Strosberg, said: "We flocked to him like settlers. He was our land."

For the practice of law, Lamek joined Fraser, Beatty, later moving to the firm that eventually became Genest Murray DesBrisay Lamek. Lamek made his mark as a general counsel, his touch for the dramatic and his ease in expressing himself

Throughout his career, Lamek kept himself deeply involved in the business of his profession. He served on the executive of virtually every organization that touched on lawyers and their activities: the Medico-Legal Society, the York County Law Association, the Canadian Bar Association, and the Lawyers' Club.

in direct and unequivocal fashion guaranteeing that he caught the attention of judges and opposing counsel. But his talents reached an even wider audience when he served with distinction as counsel for two highly publicized commissions.

The first of the commissions was conducted in the early 1980s by Mr. Justice Sam Grange, inquiring into the mysterious deaths of babies at the Hospital for Sick Children. The second commission, a decade later, came under Mr. Justice Horace Krever, as he investigated the issue of tainted blood in transfusions – a calamity that cost many citizens their health or their lives. Both commissions combined elements of complex technology and charged emotions, and it was Lamek's enormous capacities for clarity of expression and steadiness of purpose that helped to keep the commissions on track to their difficult goals. At the same time, since both hearings, particularly those of the Grange Commission, received extensive television coverage, Lamek became a familiar figure to Canadian viewers. One of his fellow counsel observed that Lamek was, for a while, "probably the most recognizable lawyer in the country."

Throughout his career, Lamek kept himself deeply involved in the business of his profession. He served on the executive of virtually every organization that touched on lawyers and their activities: the Medico-Legal Society, the York County Law Association, the Canadian Bar Association, and the Lawyers' Club. During two of his busiest years as a counsel, 1993 to 1995, he occupied the treasurer's office at a period when the Law Society was confronting severe issues with its budget and the workings of the Legal Aid Plan. Lamek remained indefatigable in pursuing solutions.

When diabetes brought the loss of a leg, Lamek hardly missed a beat. He bought a motorized scooter, on which he swooped down streets and courthouse corridors, his trade-mark scarf sailing in the breeze that he left in his speedy wake. As a young man, Lamek had set as his ultimate goal an appointment to the bench. That ambition was realized in 1999 when he became a judge of the Superior Court of Justice. It was a great misfortunate for the profession and the public that an early death two years later cut short Lamek's career in the judiciary.

Acknowledgments

The Honourable R. Roy McMurtry, *Chief Justice of Ontario*

Jeffrey Miller, *Publisher, Irwin Law*

Jack Batten, *Author*

The Osgoode Society

Great Library of the Law Society of Upper Canada

Larry A. Banack, *Chair, Law Foundation of Ontario*

The Young Advocates' Committee of The Advocates' Society

Archives of Ontario

The Advocates' Society is especially grateful to family, colleagues, and friends who provided biographical information and photographs of our fifty Learned Friends.

Project Coordinator:

Sonia Holiad, *Director of Marketing & Communications, The Advocates' Society*

Author's Acknowledgments

For recollections, memories, and other information about the counsel who are profiled in this book, I am indebted to their friends, families, former partners, and juniors who were unfailingly generous in answering my questions and providing news clippings and other written material. In some cases, it was the counsel themselves who were just as open and generous in talking about their own careers in the law. Two professional archivists were patient and tireless in digging up valuable material for the profiles: Susan Lewthwaite, Research Co-ordinator, The Law Society of Upper Canada Archives, and Barbara Taylor, Archivist, the Archives of Ontario. To all, I am most grateful.

Publisher's Acknowledgments

Irwin Law is most grateful to The Advocates' Society for inviting us to join in this very special project. We would also like to acknowledge the author, Jack Batten, for lending his unique voice to these profiles and Rosemary Shipton for her prodigious editorial skill. Paul Leatherdale, Archivist at The Law Society of Upper Canada Archives, provided invaluable assistance in tracking down many of the wonderful photographs included in this book.

Photo Credits & Sources

Cyril Frederick Harshaw Carson	2	Credit: Charles Aylett. Photo courtesy of The Law Society of Upper Canada.
	3	Credit: Canada Pictures. Photo courtesy of The Law Society of Upper Canada.
Isadore Levinter	4	Credit: Donald McKague. Photo courtesy of Benjamin Levinter.
	5	Credit: Farmer Bros. Photo courtesy of The Law Society of Upper Canada.
William Belmont Common	6	Credit: George Freeland. Photo courtesy of The Law Society of Upper Canada.
Joseph Sedgwick	8	Credit: The Telegram. Photo courtesy of The Law Society of Upper Canada.
	9	Credit: George Freeland. Photo courtesy of The Law Society of Upper Canada.
Vera Lillian Parsons	10	Credit: Lyonde and Sons. Photo courtesy of The Law Society of Upper Canada.
Margaret Paton Hyndman	12	Credit: Elliott & Fry: London, England. Photo courtesy of The Law Society of Upper Canada.
	13	Credit: Ashley and Crippen. Reprinted with permission.
Ernest Cecil Facer	14	Credit: George Freeland. Photo courtesy of The Law Society of Upper Canada.
	15	Photo courtesy of Sheila Thomson.
Roydon Ambrose Hughes	16	Photo courtesy of Donnell Hughes.
	17	Credit: George Freeland. Photo courtesy of The Law Society of Upper Canada.
Mayer Lerner	18	Photo courtesy of Mark Lerner.
	19	Photo courtesy of Mark Lerner.
John Josiah Robinette	20	Photo courtesy of the Robinette family.
	21	Credit: George Freeland. Photo courtesy of The Law Society of Upper Canada.
Francis Andrew Brewin	22	Credit: Randolph MacDonald. Photo courtesy of The Law Society of Upper Canada.
	23	Photo courtesy of the Brewin family.
Edson Livingston Haines	24	Credit: Lyonde and Sons. Photo courtesy of The Law Society of Upper Canada.
	25	Photo courtesy of Bruce Haines, JD, QC.
Bernard Cohn	26	Photo courtesy of David M. Cohn.
	27	Photo courtesy of David M. Cohn.

Brendan O'Brien	28	Photo courtesy of Mr. & Mrs. Brendan O'Brien.
	29	Credit: Charles Aylett. Photo courtesy of The Law Society of Upper Canada.
John Douglas Arnup	32	Credit: Kenneth Jarvis. Reprinted with the permission of WeirFoulds LLP.
	33	Credit: Douglas Paisley. Photo courtesy of The Law Society of Upper Canada.
Dalton Gilbert Dean	34	Photo courtesy of Diana Young.
Gordon Fripp Henderson	36	Reprinted with the permission of The Law Society of Upper Canada.
	37	Credit: Lyonde and Sons. Photo courtesy of The Law Society of Upper Canada.
Henry Herbert Bull	38	Photo courtesy of the Crown Attorney's Office, Toronto.
	39	Credit: Ashley and Crippen. Photo courtesy of The Law Society of Upper Canada.
Goldwin Arthur Martin	40	Reprinted with the permission of The Law Society of Upper Canada.
	41	Credit: Ashley and Crippen. Photo courtesy of The Law Society of Upper Canada.
John Thomas Weir	42	Photo courtesy of WeirFoulds LLP.
	43	Credit: Ashley and Crippen. Photo courtesy of The Law Society of Upper Canada.
John Mirsky	44	Photo courtesy of Peter Mirsky.
	45	Credit: Ashley and Crippen. Photo courtesy of The Law Society of Upper Canada.
John Malcolm Robb	46	Credit: Ashley and Crippen. Photo courtesy of The Law Society of Upper Canada.
Willard Zebedee Estey	48	Credit: Library and Archives Canada. Unknown photographer. Reprinted with permission.
	49	Photo courtesy of The Law Society of Upper Canada.
McLeod Archibald Craig	50	Reprinted with the permission of The Law Society of Upper Canada.
Allan Goodman	52	Photo courtesy of the Hon. Susanne Goodman.
	53	Credit: George Freeland. Photo courtesy of The Law Society of Upper Canada.
Charles Leonard Dubin	54	Photo courtesy of the Hon. Charles Dubin.
	55	Reprinted with the permission of The Law Society of Upper Canada.
Walter Bernard Williston	56	Photo courtesy of The Advocates' Society.
	57	Credit: Lyonde and Sons. Photo courtesy of The Law Society of Upper Canada.
Arthur Edward Martin Maloney	58	Photo courtesy of Ombudsman Ontario.
	59	Credit: George Freeland. Photo courtesy of The Law Society of Upper Canada

Sydney Lewis Robins	60	Reprinted with the permission of The Law Society of Upper Canada.
	61	Credit: George Freeland. Photo courtesy of The Law Society of Upper Canada.
David Gondran Humphrey	62	Reprinted with the permission of The Law Society of Upper Canada.
	63	Credit: The Studio, Edmund Soame. Photo courtesy of The Law Society of Upper Canada.
Bert James MacKinnon	64	Reprinted with the permission of The Law Society of Upper Canada.
Charles Terrence Murphy	66	Photo courtesy of Karen Barsanti/Aline Foster, Superior Court of Justice, Sudbury.
John Patrick Nelligan	68	Credit: Julie Matus. Reprinted with the permission of The Law Society of Upper Canada.
	69	Credit: Ashley and Crippen. Reprinted with permission.
Fernand Laurent Gratton	72	Credit: Brian Toll Studio. Photo courtesy of the Hon. Jean-Marc Labrosse.
	73	Credit: The Studio, Edmund Soame. Photo courtesy of The Law Society of Upper Canada.
Bernard William Hurley	74	Credit: Brian Toll Studio. Reprinted with permission.
	75	Credit: The Studio, Edmund Soame. Photo courtesy of The Law Society of Upper Canada.
Julia Verlyn LaMarsh	76	Photo courtesy of The Judy LaMarsh Fund.
	77	Copyright: Library and Archives Canada/Credit: Ron Roels/PA-117097. Reprinted with Permission.
Phillip Barry Chaytor Pepper	78	Photo courtesy of The Advocates' Society.
	79	Photo courtesy of The Law Society of Upper Canada.
John Douglas Bowlby	80	Credit: The Spectator Collection, Hamilton Public Library. Reprinted with permission.
	81	Credit: John Palmer. Photo courtesy of The Law Society of Upper Canada.
John Francis Howard	82	Photo courtesy of John Howard.
	83	Credit: Ashley and Crippen. Reprinted with permission.
Alfred Anthony Petrone	84	Credit: Thunder Bay Chronicle-Journal. Reprinted with permission. Photo courtesy of John Hornak.
	85	Credit: Ashley and Crippen. Reprinted with permission.
Donald Finlay Sim	86	Credit: Stuart's Studio Photography, Richmond Hill. Photo courtesy of Keltie Sim.
	87	Photo courtesy of The Law Society of Upper Canada.